GaryNeville

GaryNeville

The Story of a Legend

Tom Oldfield

JOHN BLAKE

Published by John Blake Publishing Ltd,
3 Bramber Court, 2 Bramber Road,
London W14 9PB, UK

www.blake.co.uk

First published in hardback in 2007

ISBN: 978-1-84454-388-5

British Library Cataloguing-in-Publication Data:
A catalogue record for this book is available from the British Library.

Design by www.envydesign.co.uk

Printed in Great Britain by CPD, Ebbw Vale, Wales.

1 3 5 7 9 10 8 6 4 2

Text copyright © Tom Oldfield, 2007

Photographs courtesy of Rex Features, Getty Images,
Empics, Clevamedia and Action Images

Papers used by John Blake Publishing are natural, recyclable products
made from wood grown in sustainable forests. The manufacturing processes
conform to the environmental regulations of the country of origin.

To Melissa, John, Veronica and Matthew
and in memory of Richard Oldfield

Contents

Introduction

You cannot begrudge Gary Neville's success as a footballer. With over 500 appearances for Manchester United to his name, he has outlasted many more illustrious team-mates and has a trophy cabinet that speaks volumes for his achievements as a player. He is the perfect role model for any young player seeking to discover how far sheer determination and dedication can take them.

Neville's path into professional football was not mapped out for him. He had to fight with everything he had for his contract at United. The fact that he has come so far in the game should be credited as much to his hard work as to his natural ability. Football has always been at the forefront of Neville's life and United cannot have had many players who love the club as much as he does.

It is rare in modern football for a player to spend his entire career at one club, but in Neville's case it is impossible to imagine him wearing the colours of any other team.

Neville has had the privilege of growing up in football alongside both his brother and his closest friends. Gary, Phil, David Beckham, Paul Scholes and Nicky Butt – not to mention those who did not make it into the first team – formed a very close-knit group, and the good fortune of going to work every day with his brother and his friends is not lost on Gary.

He knows that he is living the dream, but he will never rest on his laurels. He has earned a fortune playing football, but has never been flashy with it. He has won numerous medals, but is never complacent. Winning football matches is his job and he takes the greatest pride in it, an extremely refreshing outlook when compared to the behaviour of some professional footballers.

Everything about Neville is thoroughly professional. He lives a quiet life off the pitch, far from the newspaper headlines, trains hard, often setting aside extra time to work on his game, and has been as consistent a defender as the Premiership has seen over the past decade. Gary is a manager's dream and it comes as no surprise that Neville and Ferguson have always enjoyed a harmonious working relationship. In fact, all his managers, from Sir Alex Ferguson to Kevin Keegan and Sven-Goran Eriksson, have only praise for what Gary has achieved and for what he brings to the team.

Beginning the 1995–96 season as a first-team regular, Neville joined an elite group of players and, eleven years later, he is still occupying the right-back slot at one of the world's most famous clubs. He has won a Champions League final, five FA Cup-winners' medals and six Premiership titles. At international level, he has represented England at three European Championships and two World Cups. The big target of 100 England caps still looms large on the horizon.

He has made a name for himself with the media, too. Regularly acting as a spokesperson for Manchester United and England, Neville has made a positive impression as one of football's most articulate figures. In interviews and at press conferences he always gives an honest, realistic assessment of events and his commitment and passion shine through in his comments. Never afraid to discuss controversial topics, he will speak up if there is something bothering him and he has shown his willingness to stand by his colleagues in difficult situations. There is little more that you could ask of him as a team-mate. Now that he is the United captain, he deals with the press on an even more regular basis, but his experiences over the years have stood him in good stead.

Neville has had an outstanding career at Old Trafford and, having once been the youngster making his way in the intimidating United dressing-room, he is now the old, experienced professional who sets an example to his colleagues. As captain at Old Trafford, he, more than anyone else, *is* Manchester United. His background and his devotion mean that the club is at the core of everything he does – on and off the pitch. He has made the right full-back position his own, not only for Manchester United but also for England. His levels of consistency and fitness have enabled him to be an important team player for club and country throughout his career and he has several more years at the top ahead of him.

Compared to his best friend David Beckham, Gary's life has been less controversial and less glamorous, but Neville will always be remembered favourably at United as the local lad who fulfilled his dreams at his boyhood club and who brought home the silverware to prove it.

Chapter 1

Childhood

Gary Alexander Neville was born on 18 February 1975 to Jill and Neville Neville. He was their first child and twins Phil and Tracey followed in 1977.

All of the Nevilles are talented sports players. Gary and Phil have both reached the highest levels in football, while Tracey is an England international at netball. As teenagers, the Neville brothers were also outstanding cricketers. Both boys enjoyed cricket and Phil was considered by many to have had the same potential as Andrew Flintoff, who has since become a national cricketing hero. Gary and Phil's parents were also skilled athletes: Neville played cricket in the local Bury league, while Jill got involved in football and at one stage played as a winger. So sport was very much in the genes for Gary and his interest in all ball games became apparent at an early age.

Gary's love for football developed in primary school where he first became involved with the sport, playing football in the playground with his friends. It was not long before he was taking part in organised team football and competing against players several years older. He played for an under-11s team at the age of seven and the experience served him well for a career in football. Despite being thrown in at the deep end, the young Neville learned many important lessons, particularly when it came to the physical side of the game.

It was through his primary school that Gary gained his big break in football and his first contact with his favourite team, Manchester United. His name was put forward for a trial at United and, despite the fierce competition for places, he was one of the sixteen youngsters selected for the under-11s at the School of Excellence. He modestly says: 'Somehow someone saw something and I was selected.' He was also involved with both Bury and Greater Manchester schoolboys, and attended a Bury FC soccer school at Peel College, which allowed him to mix with people of all ages and all levels of footballing ability. Some were serious players, while others had simply been dropped off for babysitting. At that age – Neville was about ten – it taught him valuable new skills and enabled him to continue his enjoyment of the sport.

Leaving primary school, Gary and Phil went on to Elton High School in Bury. As a Manchester United fan, these were tough times for Gary. In an era dominated by

Liverpool, it took a brave man to stand up for his local team and the resentment that simmered from those school days would stay with Gary throughout his career. The roles have since been reversed but, back then, most United fans grew up despising Liverpool because of all their success. Neville and his fellow United fans could only look on as Liverpool dominated the late seventies and early eighties, winning trophies both domestically and in Europe. The Liverpool fans used to goad Gary over these triumphs – a bitter memory of his school days in Bury. Liverpool Football Club would always be a great football enemy and, with United often enjoying success over Liverpool during Neville's years in the team, Gary often found it hard to contain his delight at the lack of Premiership titles at Anfield.

The School of Excellence, which Gary entered as a ten-year-old, was his first involvement with coach Eric Harrison, who would later take charge of Manchester United's youth team. Harrison will always be remembered for bringing through an outstanding crop of players into the first team. David Beckham has called him the best youth-team coach in the country. Neville trained at the School of Excellence every Thursday and progressed as a goal-scoring midfielder. He has positive memories of the training set-up. As he recalled on the BBC website: 'The coaching was very technical at that age; there was no tactical part until the age of fifteen. It was all passing drills, five-a-sides, building up your touch and they were great times.' It made football fun for the youngsters and gave them the grounding they needed for their elevation to the first team.

Harrison takes great pride in the talented group he oversaw as youngsters. He holds Neville in very high esteem, pays tribute to Gary's qualities on and off the field and remembers him as a player who could read the game excellently. Neville still sees Harrison occasionally and is always quick to offer his help and time with any of Harrison's worthwhile causes.

Asked about what it takes to break through the youth ranks, Harrison points to the 'two Ds'. Neville was frequently told that to achieve his ambition of breaking through into the first team squad he needed 'desire' and 'dedication'. These mental attributes might not seem as crucial as ball skills, but there is no doubting Harrison's approach. He ensured that Neville and his fellow youngsters were fully prepared both physically and mentally for what was to come in their football career.

Harrison was clearly impressed with the mental attributes that Neville brought to the set-up and he has since described him as the most dedicated player he has ever worked with. While Neville has always been committed to his career, Harrison is generally believed to have instilled in him the notion that with whole-hearted devotion to his game he could become an established top-flight player.

Though Neville started hesitantly, he blossomed into a very reliable player. Gary was slow to realise that he was good enough for United and had serious doubts over his chances of making it when he was eleven and twelve. But the next few years were crucial. His devotion to his football saw him mature and develop into not only a good player, but also a leader. Back then, Harrison called Neville a 'mini-Tony Adams', a high compliment considering Adams' reputation as a brilliant motivator and organiser. Gary has brought those same qualities with him into the first team and is often seen barking out instructions to his team-mates.

While enjoying his football, Gary also played regularly for Greenmount in the Bolton Cricket League. He can even claim to have scored a century in a partnership with Matthew Hayden, the prolific Australian opening batsman. Tony Horrocks, a club stalwart at Greenmount, heaped praise on Neville's performance that day: 'Gary's century was one of the best I've ever seen in the league.' Hayden remembers both Neville brothers, with whom he socialised a fair bit. Gary and Phil were only young at the time, but they clearly impressed him with their ability: 'Phil was good, they both were. Gary was a pugnacious little cricketer, really competitive. You could definitely see more of the footballer in him than Phil, who was quietly competitive.'

Gary and Phil obviously take a lot of pride in their achievements on the cricket field. David Lloyd, at one time the England coach, considered them the best players in their age groups. Ian Botham, too, refers to them in *The Botham Report*, as two good players that got away. Clearly talented, Gary and Phil played a lot of youth cricket. Phil jokes that their dad had hoped Gary would play for Manchester United, while he (Phil) would go on to play cricket for Lancashire. But, ultimately, both brothers' futures would lie with football rather than cricket, and with Manchester United rather than Lancashire.

For Gary, that decision would come sooner than he might have expected. As luck would have it, Gary's century for Greenmount was reported in the local newspaper, the *Bury Times*. News soon reached Alex Ferguson, who had already banned Gary from playing cricket during the football close season. That was the end of it. From then on Ferguson ensured that Neville obeyed his instructions to the letter and, as a result, Gary never appeared for Greenmount again. His cricketing days were over, but at least he had the satisfaction of bowing out in style, with a century to his name.

It was not so much the money but the atmosphere that drove the Nevilles to the large white ball rather than the small red one. Playing cricket in front of tiny crowds could never compare to the vast number of spectators at youth football matches, especially schoolboy internationals. The country's passion was football and Gary knew that was where his future lay.

Having decided that his ambition was to become a professional footballer, Gary set about putting in the practice to make his dream a reality. Making his mark was no easy task as the level of competition at a club such as Manchester United was immense. He says: 'I still wonder why I was invited back every year and it can only have been attitude.' His attitude was certainly a major factor in his progress at the club. He would arrive early for training, kicking a ball against a wall until the other youngsters arrived, and his enthusiasm was there for all to see. When he saw the competition presented by the likes of local boys Paul Scholes and Nicky Butt, however, as well as the 'out-of-town' lads such as David Beckham and Robbie Savage, Gary became increasingly anxious. He was still playing as a central midfielder and the level of quality in that position made Neville fear he did not have a future at the club. Gary had played against Paul Scholes and Nicky Butt in the local league and he doesn't recall his midfield tussles against the pair with much relish! It seems that the tenacity Scholes and Butt display on the field now was already part of their make-up at a young age. Neville remembers the bruises all too clearly from the days when he faced the two tough midfielders.

Gary realised very early on that if he was going to make it, if he was going to achieve his goal, then he would have to devote himself entirely to his quest. This great maturity, even as a young man, has always been characteristic of Neville and he is fully aware of how cruel the football profession can be. As he told the BBC website: 'Three of every four lads that come into the game at the age of sixteen are out of the game by twenty.' Youngsters often leave school at sixteen to pursue a career in football only to find that a few years later they have been released and do not have enough qualifications to fall back on. John Sharples was one youngster who trained with Neville at United, but sadly his dream did not come true. He is one of so many young footballers who failed to make the grade at Old Trafford and he is now coaching the Manchester City women's team.

Neville appreciates that a career in football does not just fall into your lap and that you can never take anything for granted. He had to put in hours of extra training and fitness work to make the grade; work which mostly goes unnoticed by the general public, few of whom can really understand the challenges that young players like Gary have to overcome in order to gain a first-team contract.

Neville's path into professional football at Manchester United was far from straightforward, but his determination carried him along. He had to make decisions that alienated himself from other people his age. Surrounded by so many talented players, Gary quickly realised what was required of him – he had to make sacrifices to keep up with the other young players, who he deemed to have greater ability. After he left school at sixteen, he decided to cut himself off from his friends. It was a big moment for him and, while it seems harsh, he was aware that they would be getting up to 'all sorts of teenage things that I couldn't get involved with, even if it was just having a few drinks in Bury'. He claims that he did not go out during the two years of his apprenticeship and that he did not touch an alcoholic drink in that period. His philosophy was simple: eat, sleep and drink football.

To many youngsters this sacrifice might seem incomprehensible, but Neville has always been a strong-willed character, and his ruthless desire to succeed enabled him to cope with any restrictions he had to put on his social life during his teenage years. Neville knew that it could all end in tears, that it was a huge risk to concentrate on a career in football at only sixteen years of age, but he was reassured by the words of Alex Ferguson, who told his young players that if they could make the grade at United, they would be set up for life with the fame and fortune that comes with a successful career in Premiership football.

Neville's education in football continued when he became a full-time apprentice at Old Trafford, earning £29.50 a week. This was a lot tougher than his previous commitments. He found a world of hard graft, a world where everyone, having enjoyed their time at Old Trafford so much up to that point, was desperate not to be released. He was fighting for a professional contract. Training took place for about two hours in the morning and again in the afternoon. The whole experience was exhausting, but Neville earned the contract he craved and acknowledged that, while ability is of course crucial, luck plays a major role for a lot of players. During his apprenticeship, Neville gave everything he had to ensure he made progress at United. As he explains in his season diary *For Club and Country*, 'My attitude was that if it worked out, then good; if it didn't, I'd have no regrets.' He could not bear to look back in five years' time and wish he had tried a bit harder and so he pushed himself all the more to become a professional footballer.

Neville was also lucky to enjoy the full support of his family. The Nevilles were not wealthy. During his childhood, Gary lived in a modest terraced house looking out onto a main road and did not have a lot of money. Nevertheless, his parents made sure that he, Phil and Tracey never wanted for anything, particularly when it came to sports equipment. Clearly, his parents were important influences on young Gary. He recalls how his dad had told him: 'You've got two years to give it a real go. Never look back and wish you had done more.'

There would always be time to go back and do A-levels or university degrees. As Gary explains: 'Phil and I wouldn't be professional footballers if it hadn't been for the support of our parents.' Success has allowed both brothers to repay that debt of gratitude and to ensure that their parents now live comfortably. The brothers knew it was the very least they could do to show their gratitude.

While Neville may have focused his attention on a career in football, it does not mean that the value of a good education is lost on him. In 2002, he and his brother Phil added their support to a campaign urging youngsters to make the most of an education at comprehensive schools. Having attended a comprehensive school, the Neville brothers were asked to speak out and offer positive memories from their school days. Gary told the BBC News website: 'School for me was a great part of my childhood and has given me invaluable experiences that I'll carry with me throughout my life.' The 'comprehensive champions' scheme also recruited author Zadie Smith and MEP Glenys Kinnock. For the Nevilles, involvement was their way of giving something back to the community.

For all his efforts on the field, in his younger days Gary was never rated as highly as his peers and could not break into his county team, while his brother Phil was off playing for England Schoolboys. But rather than let such disappointments get the better of him, Gary became even more determined to make it in football. He now has the luxury of being able to look back and say 'I proved you wrong'. But there is no doubt the rejection gave him an even greater desire to succeed. Even Harrison, his coach, was initially sceptical. In his autobiography *The View from the Dugout*, he said: 'I am the first to admit that, for the first two years, I did not think he would make the grade. He had the basic skills, but was not technically good enough.'

Yet the youth coach noticed significant improvements due to Neville's work ethic and, over the next two years, found his opinion of the youngster's prospects changing. Harrison even picked the sixteen-year-old Neville as captain of the youth team ahead of seventeen- and eighteen-year-old candidates – a very rare occurrence. From then on, Harrison felt assured that Neville 'would be a first-team player and an international footballer' and cited him as an example to any youngster hoping to make it in football. The effort levels required simply to keep up at Old Trafford are extremely demanding and Neville had to put everything into each and every training session. On top of the official training, a large amount of voluntary work is expected on the training pitches and in the gym on a regular basis throughout the week. If a player fails to make it at the club, it is rarely through a lack of effort.

Manchester United is one of the biggest clubs in the world, if not the biggest, so it is to be expected that aspiring young players must give every ounce of effort to be a part of it. It is a dream for so many youngsters, and hopefuls flock from all over the country in a bid to win a contract at United. The club has its own set-ups across the country, monitoring promising footballers, and there are a number of United School of Excellence centres. Strict attention is also paid to young players' diets. The players receive instructions on what to eat and drink and, provided they follow the guidelines, they will remain at the peak of fitness. But there is little leniency for those who try to combine their football with all-night partying and heavy drinking. Neville understood that going out and drinking was not acceptable, especially as it was a waste of all the strenuous fitness work the club was putting the players through. Though it seems unbelievable to supporters that anyone would risk throwing away a career in football because of drugs or heavy drinking, it has happened many times in the past and will no doubt happen again in the future.

The attachment that Harrison developed towards young players like Neville has not been publicised enough. He was devoted to seeing his youngsters blossom in the first team, despite interest from figures such as Bryan Robson. Robson offered Harrison a coaching role at Middlesbrough, but Harrison could not desert the young players, such was the closeness he had developed with Neville and his fellow youth-team members. Harrison wanted to be on hand to see the impact of the likes of Neville, Ryan Giggs and Paul Scholes in the first team. Although it was flattering for Harrison to receive such an offer from Robson – the pair already knew each other from Robson's United days – a move away from United was never on the cards.

While Harrison has been full of praise for Neville's efforts in the youth team, Gary is equally grateful for the impact his coach has had on his career. He is adamant that without Harrison's influence he would not have made it as a professional footballer. Harrison's guidance, particularly on the art of defending, was crucial to Gary's development. By this stage, Neville had been converted to a defender, but he did not enjoy tackling – something Harrison demanded he put right. Gary had great respect for him from the word go and, while he hated to be on the receiving end of Harrison's criticism, he treasured compliments from his coach. Harrison has since left his role as youth-team coach, although he makes occasional appearances on the training ground and is still involved with scouting. Gary has said on more than one occasion that it is a great shame the young players coming through now are missing out on Harrison's wisdom and expertise. Harrison has certainly been a hugely important figure in United's success in the Premiership and was very popular with everyone he worked with.

*****

Neville's apprenticeship saw him playing in the Manchester United youth team between 1991 and 1993. It was at this time that Gary met other young hopefuls, some of whom would remain friends for life; one young Londoner would make a particular impact on Neville. This was the start of the friendship between Gary and David Beckham. The two developed a bond that has stayed strong to this day, despite the latter's move to Real Madrid. As Hunter Davies, biographer of Dwight Yorke, points out: 'They could hardly be more different. Gary is dour, canny, northern. Becks is glamorous, showy, southern.' But the two players get on well and have always spent a lot of time together off the field.

Neville and Beckham's friendship, however, was not instantaneous. Beckham arrived at Old Trafford from one of the out-of-town United centres and found himself surrounded by youngsters who had grown up together at the club. It took time for Beckham to adapt to life in Manchester. In his autobiography *My Side*, he explains that, initially, he didn't click with the local lads like Neville: 'I wasn't aware of it at the time but I think, to start with, they weren't sure about me at all: Gary says they had me down as a right flash little cockney.' Beckham would always have the best kit and initially he failed to win over his team-mates. Ultimately, however, the whole group were united by their love for football and their burning desire to represent Manchester United. As the players spent more time together, the friendship between Neville and Beckham blossomed. The two families had similar backgrounds and in Beckham, Gary had found a friend who was as committed to making it at United as he was – they were both diehard United fans.

The huge significance of football in Gary's life as a young man dictated his decision-making and he missed out on certain aspects of teenage life. But he had made up his mind that football was his future. Years later Andy Cole, the former Manchester United forward, would offer the greatest compliment to Neville's commitment. In his autobiography *Andrew Cole*, Cole says that Gary had 'devoted every element of his life to being a professional footballer' and that 'nobody could have given more'. It is generally accepted at United that Neville did not have the natural talent to glide easily into first-team football, but everyone at the club admires the dedication he has shown to make his mark in the game at the highest level.

The Manchester United youth team in which Gary played conquered all before them on the way to their 1992 FA Youth Cup triumph. Their 6–3 aggregate victory over Crystal Palace in the final thrust the team into Alex Ferguson's thoughts and a number of the youth squad quickly made the step up into the first team. While Gary is quick to claim he was carried along by the quality of the rest of the youth team, this modesty, though typical of Gary, should not mask his excellent contribution to the side at the heart of the defence. Neville and his fellow young hopefuls made Eric Harrison's job immensely enjoyable. Their coach would relish the Saturday morning matches and the opportunity to work with such a talented crop of young players. Harrison's delight at the players' potential led to several conversations with Alex Ferguson, in which he praised his young charges and urged the United boss to give them a chance. Ferguson assured his youth-team coach that the youngsters would taste first-team action in due course.

The obvious talents of Nicky Butt, Paul Scholes and David Beckham, precipitated Gary's decision to make the switch from central midfield to central defence, where he formed an excellent partnership with Chris Casper. Casper – who never quite made the grade at United – and Neville have remained in touch ever since. Although lacking the height expected of a central defender, Gary prospered in this position, but with the partnership of Steve Bruce and Gary Pallister looking so imperious and with Denis Irwin proving as consistent a left-back as you could find in the country, Gary knew that only the right-back position was attainable in the near future. So Neville determinedly set about making the transition from centre-back to right-back, learning the different skills he would need for that position. As it happened, an injury to Paul Parker would thrust Gary into the team sooner than he could possibly have anticipated.

Though he would never cement a place in the centre of United's defence, manager Alex Ferguson certainly saw the qualities Neville could bring to that position. He once remarked that if Neville was an inch taller he would be the best central defender in Britain. There is no doubt that Neville is equipped in many ways for the centre-back position. His strength in the tackle, his organisation and his close marking mean that he has all the essential attributes to play in the centre of the defence. But, as things turned out, Neville would prove the best English right-back of his generation and would make the position his own at both club and international level.

Despite the rapid progress Gary was making at United, he always remained very level-headed. His family background was a great help because his parents were down-to-earth and it was important for Neville to stay close to his roots. His family also knew the football world. Jill and Neville Neville both worked at Bury

Football Club and, albeit at a lower level, they had experience in football matters. Neville has since left his role as commercial director, but Jill still works at Gigg Lane as the club secretary. Thus, they were able to offer Gary – and later Phil – excellent guidance on how to behave as a professional footballer.

When reflecting on Gary's early days in football, it is hard to escape the fact that he was able to move through his childhood with friends who would follow him into the first team. Training full time together and encouraged by Harrison to spend as much time together as possible, the players developed an incredible bond. In his autobiography, Harrison highlights the importance of team spirit in a player's development: 'The dressing-room on training days is their second home and I rarely went into it from Monday to Friday because they grow up together in there.' These experiences made Neville and his team-mates a strong group both on and off the field. They have shared the same experiences in football and that inevitably binds them closely. For all the graft of those early years, Gary can certainly look back fondly on the lasting friendships he made during his apprenticeship at Old Trafford.

Their days as young professionals included nights out in Manchester and on such occasions Neville was always on hand to make the sensible decisions and avoid trouble. As Beckham recalls: 'We had Gary with us, who's one of the most paranoid people ever. He'd drive us mad sometimes. We'd all walk into a place, then turn round and see Gary, standing there bolt upright. "No, lads. I'm not comfortable here. We've got to get out." All it would take would be one funny look from someone. In a way it was good, because we never had a whiff of trouble.'

One name rarely mentioned when referring to the young players of Neville's youth team is Ben Thornley. Thornley is a good friend of Gary and, for a time, Neville went out with Ben's sister, Hannah. However, Thornley's life was changed when he suffered a bad cruciate ligament injury; it proved a major setback in his bid for a first-team place. This was a very sad moment in Gary's career – a moment he classes not far behind Phil's exclusion from England's World Cup '98 squad. It was very painful for Neville to see his friend's hopes crushed by the injury. Having taken such a gamble by choosing a career in football, an injury at a young age was a cruel misfortune for Thornley. It brought home the fact that playing football for a living is a wonderful job, and Gary has never taken his privileged position for granted.

Having signed his youth-team contract eighteen months earlier, Neville had shown enough quality to persuade the club that he was a player for the future. Certainly, the fact that he could play either as a right-back or a centre-back counted in his favour, not to mention the fact that he also had experience as a central midfielder. Alex Ferguson was already thinking long term and, in Neville, he had seen a player who would represent the club for many years to come. So, in

January 1993, Gary Neville signed a professional contract with Manchester United: it signalled the realisation of his goal. He had survived the School of Excellence and his apprenticeship and was now on the brink of making the huge step up to the first team. He knew this was only the beginning but, as a lifelong United fan, he was truly living the dream.

Chapter 2

Starting out for Club and Country

The momentous occasion of Gary's Manchester United debut arrived in 1992; it all happened sooner than he could possibly have imagined. His first taste of the big stage came with a substitute appearance in the UEFA Cup first-round tie against Torpedo Moscow. Still only seventeen, it represented a major breakthrough for Neville, who only years earlier had been questioning his ability to keep up with some of his more illustrious peers. It was an experience Gary would never forget. He told the media: 'I achieved my dream that night and no one could ever take it away from me. The experience of playing at Old Trafford was unbelievable and just gave me the hunger and desire to go on and on.'

The youth system at Old Trafford had been a top priority for Alex Ferguson and Manchester United for many years, but few could have predicted the exceptional success of the 1992 youth-team players. Ferguson maintains that he saw the promising signs early on. In his autobiography *Managing My Life*, the United boss explained: 'In all my managerial career I have never been so positive about a group of young footballers as I was about those who were coming through as teenagers at Old Trafford at the beginning of the 1994–95 season.' Ryan Giggs had already stepped up to the first team and, inspired by the success the Welshman had enjoyed, the likes of Neville were pushing for promotion to the senior squad.

Neville received his first Premiership run-out for United against Coventry on 8 May at the end of their triumphant 1993–94 season. It was United's last game of the campaign and it gave Neville another taste of stepping onto the Old Trafford turf. The game finished 0–0 and will not be remembered as much of a spectacle, but for Gary it was a momentous day. The fact that Alex Ferguson had given him this chance was a clear indication that Gary was a player for the future at United and that the manager wanted to introduce Neville to first-team action slowly. Ferguson has always been very shrewd in this area; he has always allowed his young players to gain experience without letting them burn out. It is an approach Neville is quick to praise. It was essential for Gary to receive good guidance from United and Ferguson did not disappoint; the manager gave his youngsters plenty of responsibility while easing them in gently.

An injury to right-back Paul Parker during the 1994–95 season saw Neville earn a run in the starting XI. He slotted into a formidable back line alongside United legends Bruce, Pallister and Irwin, and with so many high-profile figures in the team it certainly was a baptism of fire. Neville's memory of those early years includes some tough moments. The side was packed with intimidating characters, all of whom were desperate for success. He recalls many a rollicking from Steve Bruce and Mark Hughes; from Eric Cantona he simply got the stare. When you add Roy Keane and Paul Ince into the equation, you can appreciate how testing a start it was for Neville. On top of all this, there was Alex Ferguson to contend with, too. As Gary explained in the *Times*: 'It was a hard school, but the best education imaginable.'

It was make or break for Gary. Either he knuckled down and settled into the team or he wilted under the weight of expectation at the club. Many before him, and even more since, have failed to adapt to United's ruthless desire to put in flawless performances. While many of the players with whom Neville began his career would soon leave Old Trafford, there was always the sense that new players had to maintain United's very high standards.

Peter Schmeichel was particularly tough on Gary in his early days in the first team, particularly during crossing practice. The Dane's body language alone made it clear that he did not think Gary was good enough for the club. Schmeichel was a very intimidating presence and, while it made his praise worth so much more, the goalkeeper's negativity was difficult to take. In some ways, though, it had a positive effect on Neville. Rather than becoming dispirited, he became even more determined to impress Schmeichel. On a team day out several years later, the Danish goalkeeper admitted to Gary that he had proved him wrong; it was a moment of great pride for Neville. It is no coincidence that Gary's crossing has got continually better since his early days at Old Trafford and Schmeichel's tough demeanour must take some of the credit for this. It must have greatly amused Neville in late 2006 to see the man he recalls as a fearsome goalkeeper prancing across the nation's television sets on *Strictly Come Dancing*.

The United dressing-room was an intimidating place for an inexperienced youngster. He was surrounded by successful players, all of whom were strong leaders. Schmeichel's willingness to argue with anyone in the side could only have added to the tension facing Neville, who recalls the goalkeeper even rowing with manager Alex Ferguson on a couple of occasions. But this was simply Schmeichel's way of preventing the team's standards from slipping and ensuring that young players were prepared for the demands of Premiership football.

There was undoubtedly the added pressure of entering a dressing-room with experienced Premiership players who had already won several trophies. When Neville made the step up into the first team, the squad had already clinched back-to-back Premiership titles. He found himself among legends of the game who were questioning whether youngsters such as Neville would be good enough to continue the team's winning ways. Gary would make just under twenty Premiership appearances for United in Parker's absence during the 1994–95 campaign, as well as playing in two European matches. Parker's injury nightmare allowed Neville to gain valuable experience in a team packed with star names. Interestingly, Parker had also been a central defender in his early days at Fulham and QPR but, like Neville, had been converted to a right-back when he arrived at United, due to both his height and the continued excellence of Steve Bruce and Gary Pallister.

But 1994–95 was not a season to remember for the Reds. There were certainly highlights, such as the 9–0 demolition against Ipswich (a Premiership record) and a number of wins over the top clubs but, despite a solid campaign, United lost out to Blackburn in the race for the Premiership title and therefore failed in their bid to make it three titles in a row. The title race went down to the last day. As luck would have it, Blackburn lost against Liverpool, but United could only draw at Upton Park when a win would have been enough to snatch the trophy. It was a day of great disappointment for Neville and one that he would not forget in a hurry. At that stage of his career, it was the worst week of Neville's life. He was desperate to win his first Premiership title but, as Blackburn faltered, United were unable to capitalise. The mood on the coach leaving Upton Park was so bad that Neville and his team-mates vowed never to go through such pain again.

Gary was also to experience Wembley for the first time that year as he was selected to play in the FA Cup final against Everton. United had enjoyed a good run to the final, overcoming Sheffield United, Wrexham, Leeds, QPR and then Crystal Palace in the semi-final, via a stormy replay in which Roy Keane was sent off for stamping on Gareth Southgate. Having surrendered their league title to Blackburn, the FA Cup assumed an even greater significance for the United players as they sought to avoid a trophy-less season – something they had not endured since 1991–92. But it was not to be. Everton produced a determined performance to win 1–0 with their goalkeeper Neville Southall in inspired form to keep out United's best chances. It was not the start Gary would have wanted to his career. Alex Ferguson was equally dismayed and wrote in his autobiography: 'To lose any final is painful, but to lose to a team as ordinary as Everton is just not acceptable.'

The loss of Eric Cantona for the latter part of the campaign had been a massive blow. His kung-fu kick at a Crystal Palace fan, after having already been sent off, left the club with no choice but to ban the Frenchman for the rest of the season amid calls from the public for Cantona to be sacked. He had been in excellent form and the attention generated by the incident put a dent in the team's title hopes as the media swarmed around the club. He had been scoring consistently and, although

Andy Cole had been signed from Newcastle for £7 million, it was impossible to replace what the mercurial Frenchman brought to the United side.

Fortunately for Gary, this initial heartbreak was not to become a feature of his time with his boyhood team. The 1995–96 season saw United put down a marker for the rest of the decade and showed that they had the most talented squad in the country. His future at United still far from certain, Neville looked on anxiously as Alex Ferguson embarked on an extraordinary pre-season clear out. He had already decided that changes were required, making his mind up at the end of the previous season to sell Paul Ince. Ince headed to Inter Milan and was followed out of the Old Trafford door by Andrei Kanchelskis, who signed for Everton in a £5 million deal, and United legend Mark Hughes, who moved to Chelsea. After finishing the previous campaign empty handed, it was a bold policy from the United manager.

This led to uproar among United fans and the football world waited with bated breath to see which star names Ferguson would attract to replace those who had left. They would be disappointed, because Ferguson had seen enough in the performances of his youngsters to place his faith in them. When the new season kicked off, Neville was picked in a young team for the opening Premiership fixture at Villa Park. United lost 3–1. The press questioned Ferguson's focus and judgement and Alan Hansen blasted the United youngsters with the infamous line, 'You can never win anything with kids.' Hansen's words stung Neville and his fellow youngsters, but the opening-day defeat made them all the more determined to succeed. Eric Harrison was another onlooker saddened by the day's events. He was out scouting at Barnsley on that particular afternoon and was devastated to hear the score from Villa Park. It really hurt him to hear his young charges being written off so savagely and his scouting trip had suddenly lost its appeal. But he could not help but laugh as Hansen's words came back to bite him over the course of the season.

Despite Neville's fears that the manager would axe him, Ferguson continued with his youngsters. Looking back, he was not sure that the manager was convinced about him as a first-team player and had doubts over his chances of holding down a place in the starting line-up. But with limited options, Ferguson kept faith with his inexperienced youngsters and it quickly brought dividends. Five consecutive wins brought rave reviews and the same supporters who had previously been so scathing were now getting carried away by the talent in the team. Comparisons were inevitably made with the great Busby Babes who had brought home the European Cup in 1968.

Neville knows that he is indebted to Alex Ferguson for giving him his break in first-team football and is eternally grateful to his manager. It was Ferguson who was prepared to stake his reputation, and ultimately his job, on the potential of a group of youngsters, all of whom were untried at the highest level. He sold a series of big-name players in order to give Neville and the other fledglings a run in the team – a move few other managers would have been brave enough to make. There is no doubt that Gary owes his manager a lot for his chance to shine at the club.

Things went from strength to strength for United and the players took great delight in proving the critics wrong. The solid results had all been achieved without the team's talisman Eric Cantona, who was still serving his nine-month ban. This was a real boost, as Neville and his team-mates knew that if they could pick up points early on, they would be able to pull away once Cantona was eligible again. But first there was a UEFA Cup game to think about. United already had misgivings about this competition. Having spent the previous two years competing in the European Cup, it was a massive blow for the team to miss out to Blackburn in the Premiership. However, the manner of their first-round exit at the hands of Rotor Volgograd was rather embarrassing. The first leg finished 0–0, but United were strong favourites for the second leg at Old Trafford. It did not turn out like that, though, as their Russian opponents sneaked through on away goals following a 2–2 draw. The most memorable thing about their UEFA Cup adventure was Peter Schmeichel acrobatically scoring United's second goal at Old Trafford in a desperate last few minutes. The competition had been a disaster, but United were more focused on the

Premiership and the FA Cup and their early elimination from Europe meant they could now put all their efforts into these two competitions.

Cantona eventually returned from his ban and provided extra inspiration for the team. Amid all the talk of United's youngsters, it is easy to forget that there were still many experienced heads in the United dressing-room. Schmeichel, Irwin, Bruce and Pallister still provided a solid base at the back, while Ryan Giggs and Roy Keane had several seasons under their belts. Eric Cantona in attack was into his fourth season at Old Trafford. So although fledglings Neville, Scholes, Butt and Beckham were featuring regularly in the team, they were surrounded by plenty of veterans. As Roy Keane explained in his autobiography *Keane*: 'Contrary to the popular perception that we fielded a team of "kids", there was plenty of experience in the side. Nicky Butt and Paul Scholes had enough Premier League experience. Only Gary Neville and David Beckham properly fitted the "kids" description.'

Before long, the 'kids' were household names and were featured in newspapers and magazines across the nation. It also helped that the senior players looked out for them. Cantona, in particular, was a role model for the younger generation. Neville was awestruck by the Frenchman and the aura he carried with him. Being in the same dressing-room as Cantona was a dream come true for Neville and the skills the Frenchman possessed left Gary in awe. But the thing that caught Neville's attention most was that, despite Cantona's magical natural talent, the forward worked extremely hard on the training ground. It was a lesson in how to achieve greatness in football.

In Cantona's first match of the season, he grabbed an equaliser from the penalty-spot to spare United's blushes at home in a 2–2 draw with Liverpool. Neville and his team-mates progressed steadily through October and November, recording impressive wins over Chelsea and Southampton among others, but December proved a nightmare; United endured a very poor patch and wobbled worryingly. This was a tricky time for Neville, but ultimately it was a spell that taught him what it took to be the best. Draws with Chelsea and Sheffield Wednesday and defeats against Liverpool and Leeds put United's title challenge in jeopardy as Newcastle raced into a big lead at the top of the Premiership table. Crucial victories against Newcastle themselves and QPR put United back on track, but a 4–1 drubbing against Tottenham at White Hart Lane made it one win from the team's last six premiership away games. A home draw with Aston Villa put United even further behind Newcastle.

However, United were soon back to their best form. Neville, who was experiencing the high-stakes matches that come with the territory at United, and his fellow defenders returned to their usual impeccable standards and the wins came pouring in. West Ham, Wimbledon, Blackburn, Everton and Bolton were all beaten as

United put pressure on Kevin Keegan and his Newcastle squad. The Bolton match was a particularly stylish display as United triumphed 6–0 and set themselves up perfectly for their next match, at St James' Park against leaders Newcastle.

The Newcastle game was one of the most memorable of Gary's short career to date. As a Manchester United fan, it mattered even more to get the victory that would chip away at Newcastle's confidence. But Newcastle came out very strongly and forced Neville and his team-mates onto the back foot. After enduring periods of torrid pressure and enforced backs-to-the-wall defending, Manchester United struck on the counter-attack as Phil Neville's cross found Cantona in enough space to finish emphatically. St James' Park fell silent as Gary and his resurgent team-mates celebrated wildly. United held out for the win, and with over two months of the campaign remaining, Neville was in contention for a first Premiership-winners' medal. Meanwhile, the team's FA Cup run had almost been as impressive as their league form and the Double was still up for grabs. Manchester City were beaten in the sixth round in a memorable derby match and Southampton were defeated 2–0 in the quarter-final.

A draw in the Premiership against QPR ended United's sequence of six consecutive league wins, but four more wins in the next four games extended their unbeaten run. United's consistency was particularly significant at this stage of the season as they faced some tough opponents.

Both Arsenal and Tottenham boasted quality players – and certainly more experienced footballers than the likes of Neville and the other fledglings – but United were able to take maximum points from both games. This was to become typical of the team as year-in, year-out their form after Christmas proved phenomenal. His experiences on the team coach after the West Ham game the previous season gave Neville even more motivation for the title run-in. He told the *Sun* towards the end of the campaign: 'We are all burning up inside. We want to carry on winning. There are only seven games left now. We have got to make sure we win all of them.'

Such was the mood in the United dressing-room that draws were beginning to feel like defeats. A draw with Queens Park Rangers left a mood of dismay around the club. But confidence was restored following a gripping FA Cup semi-final against Chelsea that saw United confronted with the familiar face of Mark Hughes leading the Chelsea line. Ruud Gullit opened the scoring for the Blues, but Neville and his colleagues dug deep to fight back and win 2–1, with David Beckham grabbing the winner and providing further praise for the United youngsters. The victory set up an FA Cup final between United and their close rivals Liverpool – it was a clash that Neville would relish.

There was still plenty of work to be done in the Premiership before Neville could look ahead to a second consecutive FA Cup final appearance, but the team was in such good form that Newcastle simply could not hold onto their advantage. Wins over Manchester City and Coventry edged United closer to the trophy, but a 3–1 defeat to Southampton at The Dell ensured that the title race would go right down to the wire. Once again the Saints had proved a banana skin for Gary and his team-mates. However, United kept their nerve when it counted most and won their final three matches, two of them emphatically, to clinch a third Premiership crown in four years. Newcastle, who had made such an outstanding start to the season and who had fought so hard to take the race to the last day of the season, were left empty handed and distraught.

Alex Ferguson later spoke of his confidence that Newcastle could be overcome. As the season was reaching its most crucial stage, he saw that his own players, so savagely criticised at times during the season, were on the up, while Newcastle's bid for the title was running off the rails. Schmeichel was excelling in goal and Neville and his defensive colleagues fed off the confidence he gave to the back four, with all of them consistently making crucial contributions.

The stunning comeback staged by United denied Newcastle their first trophy since their 1955 FA Cup triumph and left the city stunned. Cantona's performances since his ban had been inspired and his winner at St James' Park tipped the balance of the title race firmly in Manchester United's favour, putting Kevin Keegan and his team on the verge of collapse.

For Keegan, unaccustomed to such dizzy heights as a

manager, it was a very hard experience. Towards the end of the campaign, he seemed to be losing control as he responded to Ferguson's mind games – he was not the first, and would not be the last, to be sucked into the United manager's games. The most famous moment came live on Sky Sports when voicing his disgust about comments Ferguson had made ahead of Newcastle's match with Leeds. Referring to the match between Middlesbrough and Manchester United on the final day of the season, he said, in a fit of anger: 'But I'll tell ya – you can tell him now if you're watching it – we're still fighting for this title, and he's got to go to Middlesbrough and get something, and I tell you honestly, I'd love it if we beat them – *love it*.' The huge pressure that comes with managing a top club had clearly taken its toll on Keegan as his title dreams were snatched away by United in the cruellest of twists.

The FA Cup final win over Liverpool put the icing on the cake for Neville and United. Although he was not picked in the starting line-up (Phil was selected ahead of him), it was a truly memorable day for Gary as he came off the bench to witness the feeling of winning a cup final at Wembley at first hand. It was an emotion that made him determined to return to the showpiece final at every possible opportunity. The game had seemed destined for extra-time after ninety minutes of stalemate, but once again it was Cantona who stepped up to rescue United. The Liverpool goalkeeper David James spilt a corner from David Beckham and the ball fell at an awkward height to Cantona, who was able to re-adjust his feet and strike the ball into the unguarded net through a sea of bodies in the penalty area. The Frenchman wheeled away in delight and was followed by all of his team-mates.

Neville's first full season in the first team had ultimately proved a huge success as he won the Premiership and FA Cup Double in an incredible campaign. He had proved himself a very talented defender and his performances would be rewarded with a place in Terry Venables' Euro '96 squad for the international tournament that summer. There had been some testing times along the way, but the manner in which he had coped with difficult situations showed Ferguson that he had the qualities to win trophies at United for years to come. Still only twenty-one, Neville undoubtedly had a very bright future ahead of him.

*****

The early part of Neville's international career saw him enter a team that had struggled badly in recent years, much to the dismay of the football-crazy nation. The shocking failure to qualify for the 1994 World Cup in the USA, which followed the team's poor performances in the 1992 European Championships in Sweden, had put English football in the doldrums, despite the roaring success of the Premiership. But England manager Terry Venables was helping to restore some pride with four wins and two draws from his first six matches in charge.

It was Venables who first picked Neville for an England squad, who gave him his first cap and who selected him for his first major tournament. Gary's performances for Manchester United during the 1994–95 seasons earned him his first cap for his country against Japan in the Umbro Trophy in the summer of 1995. England won 2–1 on the day and it was another sweet moment for Neville; it was another boyhood dream fulfilled. At the time, Neville set a new record for the fewest club appearances before earning an England cap since the Second World War. He had played only nineteen times for United prior to his first cap. Gary's arrival on the international scene also marked the end of any long summer breaks. With a World Cup or European Championship tournament every two summers and countless minor competitions and friendlies to be fitted into any available summer dates, the start of Gary's international career meant he would be playing football almost year-round.

Phil joined Gary in the England squad in early 1996 when the pair became the first brothers to be selected since Bobby and Jack Charlton. Understandably, the whole Neville family was very proud; indeed, Gary's parents were starting to become accustomed to the success of their children. While Gary and Phil were both in the England football squad, Tracey was representing England at netball. The Nevilles could legitimately claim to be the most successful sporting family in the country.

Phil made his international debut against China on 23

May 1996. Gary was also in the team that day and it handed the pair a place in the history books as only the second pair of brothers to represent England in the twentieth century. It was an achievement both brothers were delighted about. Terry Venables was full of praise for the duo. He enjoyed having the youngsters in the squad and was certainly impressed with their professionalism. He predicted that they would have long careers ahead of them at international level. Venables was turning the England team around and, with the European Championships due to be held in England in 1996, there was a feeling of anticipation sweeping across the country once more.

As hosts, England received automatic qualification and so had to content themselves with a series of friendlies as preparation for the tournament. Neville was selected in the squad and he found the passion and support of the English crowds a huge spur. For Gary, Manchester United had always been the only team in his life and it was not until he began playing regularly for England that he felt the significance of playing for his country. He used to admire individuals such as Steve Bruce, Tony Adams and Paolo Maldini because of their quality performances for their clubs rather than for their displays at international level, and so the sheer joy of representing his country was slightly lost on Gary at first. He had represented the England Under-18 squad when they won the European Youth Championships, but it was only when he pulled on the England shirt at senior level that everything sunk in for him. As he revealed in his *Times* column on 11 June 1998: 'Euro '96 really brought it home to me how important it was to so many people. I remember looking at all the faces, full of hope and willing us on, and that gave me a real buzz.'

The build-up to the tournament went smoothly for England. Neville was involved in all the warm-up matches and the team produced some impressive performances, though the standard of some of the opposition was rather weak – China and Hungary are certainly sides that England ought to be capable of beating. England were handed a reasonable group for the group stage of the tournament, drawn with Switzerland, Scotland and Holland.

In England's first match, willed on by the wild support from the nation's fans at Wembley, the team faced Switzerland, who they had beaten 3–1 in a friendly in November 1995. This time, though, the game finished 1–1. It was a match England felt they should have won, having led through an Alan Shearer first-half goal, but a Kubilay Türkyilmaz penalty, awarded for a Stuart Pearce handball, with eight minutes to go enabled Switzerland to snatch a point. It was not the start Neville would have wanted, but England were still in contention.

Next up was the grudge match against Scotland and, with a final group match against a talented Dutch team, a win was desperately needed. England used to play Scotland, Wales and Northern Ireland on a regular basis, but more recently such fixtures had been rare, despite the fact that a tournament still exists for international schoolboy football between the home nations. The fact that England and Scotland had not played each other many times in recent history added extra significance to the match at Euro '96. England got the three points with a 2–0 win at Wembley, but it could all have been very different if, with England leading 1–0, Scotland had converted a penalty, awarded for a Tony Adams foul. Unfortunately for the Scots, Gary McAllister's penalty was diverted over the bar by the elbow of England goalkeeper David Seaman. Minutes later, Paul Gascoigne provided the sucker punch at the other end with a phenomenal second goal for England as he flicked the ball over Scotland's Colin Hendry before firing a volley into the back of the net.

If Neville and his team-mates had stirred some hope among England fans with their solid start, the third and final group match had supporters firmly believing that England could take on any team in the tournament. A Holland team boasting stars such as Dennis Bergkamp, Clarence Seedorf and the De Boer brothers were mercilessly outplayed by England in a 4–1 rout. Two goals apiece from strikers Alan Shearer and Teddy Sheringham put England top of the group. For a twenty-one-year-old, the pressure and intensity of these big matches could have been unnerving, but Neville took to major tournament games with minimal fuss. Crucially, he was able to keep focused and forget about the high stakes riding on every match. He treated every match as simply another game and this attitude enabled him to handle the pressure. Obviously there were pre-match jitters, but his mature approach to his football allowed Neville to avoid being overawed by the importance of the matches.

With the nation behind them, the England players went into the quarter-final full of confidence. Their opponents, Spain, had only just qualified from their group and, despite the obvious quality of some of their players, England did not fear them. After a 0–0 stalemate during full-time and extra-time, the match was decided on penalties. Shearer, David Platt, Pearce and Gascoigne scored their spot-kicks for England, while Hierro and Nadal both missed for Spain to hand England a dramatic shootout victory. The match will always be recalled by Neville with mixed feelings. It was a truly magical day to be involved with the national team, as England put the misery of 1992 and 1994 behind them, but Neville picked up a yellow card in the game; following the yellow card he picked up against Switzerland, it meant he was suspended for the semi-final against the old enemy Germany. Now only the Germans, who had beaten Croatia in their quarter-final, stood between England and the final.

This was the biggest match for England since the shootout heartbreak against the same opponents at Italia '90, but Gary would be forced to watch the match from the touchline. After the Switzerland match – England's first of the tournament – Neville was aware of the tightrope he would be walking and he kicked himself for putting himself under added pressure. Being the honest professional he is, Gary had no complaints over the yellow card; instead he hoped he had learned from the incident. He already had experience of carrying a yellow card in his United career, so he knew how to approach the situation, but ultimately a rather extravagant tumble from Spanish full-back Sergi would bring a one-match ban for the United man.

It was tough to accept, especially as the rest of the squad was preparing for the semi-final and the nation was on cloud nine. But Terry Venables reassured him that he should be looking to the final, for which Gary would be available again. Even the disappointment of the suspension could not totally dampen Neville's enthusiasm. As soon as the referee showed him the yellow card he knew he was out of the next game, but it did not affect his performance at all as he refused to let his team-mates or the England supporters down. Gary was hurting, but the positive element was that England had reached the semi-finals and that made Neville very happy. However, the Germans had made the semi-finals with a series of solid displays and would represent the toughest test so far to the new-look England.

The semi-final could not have started better for England as they took the lead after only three minutes when a Paul Gascoigne corner was headed home by Alan Shearer for his fifth (and final) goal of the competition, enough to earn Shearer the Golden Boot. But Germany pulled level less than fifteen minutes later through Stefan Kuntz and the game remained locked at 1–1 after full-time and extra-time, despite a desperate slide in vain from Gascoigne to reach a Shearer cross. So the game went to penalties and England were forced to face their demons. The spot-kicks from both sides were immaculate, so much so that after five penalties each they were level at 5–5. Then came sudden death spot-kicks and Gareth Southgate saw his penalty kept out by German goalkeeper Andreas Köpke. Andreas Möller slotted home the decisive penalty and England's dream of a European Championship final was crushed. Germany went on to lift the trophy, beating the Czech Republic 2–1 with a golden goal from Oliver Bierhoff, his second strike of the game, in extra-time. Incidentally, this was the first-ever golden goal in a major international tournament.

Neville had to endure the frustration of being eliminated from the tournament without being able to help his team-mates. His hopes of returning for the final had been destroyed and he had felt isolated and helpless sitting on the sidelines. But when one considers Gary's age and the reliable performances he had produced, it was a month of football that he could look back upon with some satisfaction. With limited first-team experience, Neville had held his own against some of the world's finest players and he had shown all the signs of a player who would be a fixture in the England team for over a decade.

After Euro '96, Terry Venables stepped down as England manager to concentrate on upcoming legal battles, as had been arranged prior to the tournament. Glenn Hoddle, on the back of success at club level with Swindon and Chelsea, was appointed to replace Venables, and he brought a different kind of approach to the job. Having featured in fourteen of the sixteen England matches under Venables since his debut, Neville was sometimes the unlucky man to miss out during Hoddle's spell in charge as the manager sought to adopt the 3-5-2 formation, using wing-backs rather than full-backs. David Beckham and Darren Anderton were occasionally preferred to Neville on the right in that particular formation.

But Hoddle was in no doubt about Gary's ability, despite Neville's insistence at playing down his attacking qualities, and the England manager made that very clear when speaking to the media: 'I don't agree with him at all about him not being comfortable going forward. He is being nice and modest but, within himself, he is a very confident lad.' It is no coincidence that so many coaches and managers have enjoyed working with Neville.

After completing the Double in 1996, United had re-established themselves as the top club in the country and Blackburn's title success in 1995 seemed nothing more than a blip in United's period of control. But Neville and his fellow players were now taking nothing for granted. The younger players in the squad, Neville included, were still hungry for trophies. While the Premiership was again a priority, the Champions League was also a competition that United hoped to conquer.

Chapter 3

First-Team Regular

Neville signed a new five-year contract at United in September 1996. It was not a hard decision for Gary, whose love for United was already abundantly clear. After putting pen to paper, he announced: 'I would sign a ten-year contract if it was put in front of me. I just want to play for Manchester United and no other club.' Alex Ferguson knew that of all the players in his squad, negotiations with Neville and the other fledglings would probably be the most straightforward, such was their devotion to the club where they had spent their youth together.

Neither of the Neville brothers has ever had an agent, normally their dad sits in on all business deals. They see no reason to involve agents. The club has always been very fair with their dealings and Gary certainly always trusted Ferguson and the rest of the management team to put forward an acceptable offer. Having worked so hard to gain a contract at the club, Gary never had any intention to leave. He explained in his season-long diary: 'I have always preferred dealing directly with the club about my contracts. There's no good reason for us to pay a significant percentage to a third party on club and boot contracts; we know what we should be paid anyway. It would upset me if I ever had to give a penny to an agent on my club or boot contracts.' It seems too that the Nevilles and the other Fergie Fledglings were very open about their contracts. Gary and Phil always shared the terms of their deals with their fellow youngsters and were often the ones whom the others followed when it came to negotiations. Both Neville brothers began their careers with boot deals with Pony before switching to Diadora during the 1997–98 season. Since then, Gary has switched to Adidas. Certainly, while the Nevilles were both playing for United, it was common for them to sign for the same company because they were easier to market as a package. So they always tended to sign contracts as a pair.

Alex Ferguson strengthened his squad over the summer of 1996 by making a series of signings. Firstly, he brought in two unknown Norwegian players, who turned out to be sensational additions to the United team. Ronny Johnsen, a strong, quick defender, and Ole Gunnar Solskjaer, a striker with an incredible goal-scoring instinct, were brought in to bolster what was already a squad brimming with quality. Karel Poborsky, the Czech right-winger, arrived for £3.5 million from Slavia Prague on the back of an impressive tournament during Euro '96, and Jordi Cruyff, son of the great Johann, was picked up from Barcelona. In less-publicised deals, Raimond van der Gouw arrived as Peter Schmeichel's deputy, Tony Coton swapped Manchester City for Manchester United to provide extra goalkeeping cover and Wes Brown made the step up to the United first-team squad. Brown, tipped to have a big future, was the latest in a long line of talented United youth products. Following a busy summer in the transfer market, the new additions to the squad needed time to gel during pre-season.

Newcastle, runners-up in the previous campaign, were Manchester United's Charity Shield opponents and Neville and his team-mates sent out a strong message with a 4–0 win. After what had been a tight and bitter end to the 1995–96 title race, United struck a good early blow to their rivals. While these matches are never a strict guide to the season ahead, such an emphatic win would undoubtedly have made an impact on Tyneside. Neville began the match on the bench, but came on at half-time to savour the team's positive start.

The opening day was ominous for United's title challengers. An emphatic win away to Wimbledon was capped by David Beckham's famous goal, struck over Neil Sullivan from inside his own half. It was hard to believe that just a year ago, both the pundits and the general public had heaped criticism on the young United team, claiming that these very same players could not bring success to the club. A run of three consecutive draws was less impressive, but a 4–0 victory over Leeds signalled a return to winning ways. The question was: could any of the challengers maintain the consistency to stay close to United?

Gary had to remain patient as Denis Irwin and his brother Phil occupied the full-back positions. It was a difficult time, but his chance would come and he would play a big part in the team's season. An unfortunate injury to Phil against Blackburn in the team's third Premiership match gave Gary an opening at right-back and he made the most of the opportunity. United's form was good and Neville and his fellow defenders ended the month of September with two clean sheets against Aston Villa and Tottenham. Liverpool and Arsenal had both made strong starts too, and it was Liverpool who emerged as the early league leaders, with Arsenal trailing by three points and United by four.

A 1–0 defeat to Juventus in the Champions League on 11 September came as a disappointment to Neville and his team-mates as they hoped to make a greater impression on the competition. It was a strange group-stage performance from United in general as they won three and lost three to qualify on nine points, including a rare home defeat against Fenerbahce. The loss to the Turkish side was United's first in Europe for forty years, a record that included fifty-six games without defeat.

Two losses against Juventus, without scoring a goal, failed to quash the suggestions that United could not compete with the very best European clubs.

Going into the final game of the group stage against Rapid Vienna, Neville knew that if Fenerbahce won against Juventus, United would be eliminated regardless of their result. So he hoped that the team would go out and attack Rapid Vienna, producing the type of form that they had shown in the second half against Juventus in their previous European match. He knew that Fenerbahce would struggle to win in Turin and so the mood at United was very positive. Neville and his team-mates beat Rapid Vienna 2–0 and the other result went United's way. They had made it through the group and a few poor performances had not ultimately proved costly. It may not have been the type of form Neville would have hoped for, but qualification – the main objective – had been achieved.

While August and September had been solid, things were about to change in what many believe was United's shakiest pursuit of the Premiership title during the 1990s. Despite a decent start of nine matches unbeaten, United endured a miserable period in the Premiership in late October and early November. October began well enough with a 1–0 win over rivals Liverpool, but their next three Premiership games were far from memorable. Firstly, they were hammered 5–0 by a Newcastle team out for revenge at St James' Park. United then travelled to their bogey ground, The Dell, where Southampton ripped through them as emphatically as Newcastle had done as they recorded a stunning 6–3 win. To add to the team's misery, Roy Keane was sent off. A 2–1 home defeat to Chelsea completed a disastrous patch for United, who had conceded thirteen goals in three matches and who had not picked up a single point.

Ferguson described the defeat to Newcastle as the worst result of his entire managerial career and was clearly devastated. Neville himself had a torrid time against the in-form David Ginola and was responsible for allowing the Frenchman space to score Newcastle's second goal. While the poor results dented Neville's confidence, they were ultimately character-building moments. He came back stronger and wiser. Having signed no defenders over the summer, Ferguson had put his faith in the current crop and so it was up to Neville and his fellow defenders to make amends. Alex Ferguson may have been dismayed with the results, but he admitted it had been a good learning curve for his young players. He wrote in *Manchester United, The Official Review 1996–'97*: 'They were freak results, but the players still had to keep their heads and avoid the panic shown by a lot of the media. The players showed great determination and character to come back.'

A 1–0 home win over Arsenal – thanks to Nigel Winterburn's own goal – brought much needed relief for United. After their run of results, it was critical that they posted a victory to restore confidence among the players and everyone connected to the club. It proved a turning point in United's season and confidence oozed back into the side. While they picked up a few disappointing draws over the next weeks, the team did not lose again in the Premiership until 8 March. A much happier Ferguson looked back on the shaky patch as 'nightmare moments'.

This victory was the beginning of a sixteen-game unbeaten run for United in the Premiership; it was a run that resurrected their title challenge. Wins against Leeds, Tottenham and Arsenal again breathed new life into the side and secured their place at the top of the table. Sunderland were beaten 5–0 with Solskjaer and Cantona grabbing two goals each and Nicky Butt adding the fifth. United followed that result with a 4–0 victory away to Nottingham Forest with four different players on the scoresheet. An Eric Cantona goal against his former club gave United another victory as Leeds were defeated 1–0.

The one disappointment during this run came in the FA Cup at the hands of Wimbledon. After a 1–1 draw at Old Trafford, the fourth-round clash went to a replay at Selhurst Park, which Wimbledon won through a Marcus Gayle goal. United pressed desperately for an equaliser, but just could not break down the Wimbledon defence as the competition once again proved a great leveller. The FA Cup has always been special for Gary and he was pained by their early exit from the competition.

With barely a chance to catch their breath, United were soon back on the European stage. They had reached the Champions League quarter-finals – a worthy achievement – but if they really wanted to be considered a force in Europe, the team knew that further progress was required. FC Porto were United's quarter-final opponents and United were playing them at the top of their game. The first leg at Old Trafford sealed the tie as United produced one of their best European displays and their excellent 4–0 win made the second leg a formality. A 0–0 draw in Portugal cemented their place in the last four.

The German side Borussia Dortmund awaited United in the semi-finals. Neville was upbeat. It was a chance to settle a score with the Germans after the Euro '96 defeat. He told the *Sun*: 'It's about time we put one over on them and beat one of their teams, even though they have the knack of winning so much. All my life I have seen them doing that.' He recalled the Euro '96 semi-final – a game he missed through suspension – when England matched Germany stride for stride yet were still eliminated. He hoped that both England and United could show the same kind of killer instinct. Neville picked out Köhler, Riedle, Sammer, Reuter and Möller as Dortmund's dangermen. He felt that their knowledge of the big occasions – from European Cup finals and World Cup finals – was a real threat, but he also knew that United themselves had built up plenty of European know-how. Dortmund might have the experience, but United had youth on their side and, with the fledglings improving with every game, Neville hoped that United's pace would hurt their German opponents.

*****

As their title challengers faltered badly, United pressed on with solid wins away to Blackburn and Liverpool. Neville helped to set up the third goal in the 3–1 win at Anfield, as David James flapped at his cross and allowed Andy Cole to score. Eric Cantona was in sublime form and Neville marvelled at the Frenchman's performances. Cantona was the United player opposition teams were most wary of and his sheer presence was enough to strike fear into defenders all over the world. Neville told the *Sun*: 'There is not a manager who does not instruct his team to combat the threat of Cantona.'

The Frenchman was a big influence on Gary and the other youngsters. For them, Cantona was their leader and, along with other senior players, he helped the younger members of the team enjoy a smooth transition into the side. Some of the goals Cantona scored during the season were magnificent.

Liverpool were enjoying an impressive campaign but, much to Neville's delight, their defeat at home to United put a huge dent in their title aspirations. At the end of April, United had a game in hand and led the league by five points, ahead of Arsenal and Liverpool. It was going to take a miracle for Neville and his team-mates to be stopped now. But with the Premiership seemingly wrapped up, the Champions League proved a step too far for United. They lost the first leg of their semi-final away to Borussia Dortmund 1–0, but still felt confident they could turn things around at Old Trafford and realise the dream of a European final.

However, Lars Ricken, the scorer in the first leg, crushed the United dream by scoring again in the second leg and the experienced German side shut United out. Disappointed they may have been, but Neville and his team-mates could reflect on definite improvement in Europe and their first Champions League semi-final appearance. Manager Alex Ferguson was pleased with his players' efforts and post-match he told the media: 'I don't have any criticism of my players. They gave everything and I couldn't have asked for more – apart from a few goals.'

The Germans went on to lift the trophy against Juventus in the Champions League final and so, as has happened several times, United were eliminated by the eventual winners. The concern for Ferguson was that his players had failed to unlock the Dortmund defence in 180 minutes of football and clearly the team still had a bit to learn about how to achieve the highest honours in European competition. Ferguson would eventually find the right mix of attacking options to conquer the Champions League.

A solid Premiership season petered out with three draws and a win at home against West Ham. The 3–3 draw with Middlesbrough at Old Trafford was a historic day for Gary as he scored his first ever goal for the club to help United fight back for a point. It was a hugely proud moment, one of many from the season. He also supplied the cross for Solskjaer to grab the equaliser in the same game. The 2–0 victory over West Ham was a day of celebration at Old Trafford. Gary did not play, but was able to enjoy the jubilant mood as the United fans paid tribute to the team's achievements. Peter Schmeichel even spent the latter stages of the match trying to persuade Alex Ferguson to let him play as a striker.

The campaign had more low points than past and future Manchester United title successes, but the challengers failed to capitalise on several poor patches from United. The team conceded more goals than any other of the top-five clubs and lost five matches on the way to the title. The fact that they drew twelve league games is another statistic that would have slightly worried Ferguson, Neville and United. Newcastle were once again the closest challengers for the trophy, but they finished seven points behind in second, on the same total as Arsenal and Liverpool, who were third and fourth respectively. However, there were encouraging signs for the other title contenders, as United had been far from convincing at times during the season.

It had been a decent campaign for Gary, who had proved his quality both at right-back and, on a few occasions, in the centre of defence. He made forty-four starts for United during the season and had chalked up his first goal for the club. Neville knew United could perform far better than they had during patches of the season. But as United captain Eric Cantona hoisted the Premiership trophy, once again decorated with the red and white of Manchester United, it was a time to celebrate another major success rather than dwell on any of the team's shortcomings. Alex Ferguson wore a big smile as he saw his players retain the title.

For Neville, now an established member of the England set-up, there would be no lengthy summer break to re-charge his batteries. His impressive displays for United earned him a place in the squad for Le Tournoi, a tournament featuring England, Brazil, Italy and France. Early on in Hoddle's spell at the helm, Gary had missed a few internationals, but he was raring to go ahead of the tournament. Though he would be absent from part of United's pre-season, he was excited about facing three of the top sides in international football. He played in all three games of Le Tournoi, having performed well in the World Cup qualifiers. The tournament turned out to be a real boost for English football as the team finished top of the group. The results spoke for themselves. Neville and England may have lost to Brazil, but wins over France and Italy were excellent achievements and suggested that England were moving in the right direction. After winning the Premiership that season, it had been a superb year for Gary.

*****

The 1997–98 campaign began with the surprise retirement of United legend Eric Cantona. It came as a huge shock to the players, who were given no indication of Cantona's decision and were expecting him to arrive for pre-season training. The Frenchman had been phenomenal at Old Trafford and was very popular with everyone at the club. Reflecting on Cantona, Neville paints a very positive picture of his former team-mate. In *For Club and Country*, he says: 'I just remember him for the great things he did for the club. United hadn't won the championship for twenty-six years before he arrived and it's no coincidence that we finally won it in his first season here.'

Neville was told during pre-season that he and David Beckham would not feature at the beginning of the season due to the heavy workload the two players had endured over the past few seasons. Alex Ferguson feared that Gary was playing too much football, as he had not had a summer off since he broke onto the scene for United. He played in the Umbro Cup in 1995, the European Championships in 1996 and then Le Tournoi in 1997. A heavy workload it may have been, but Neville had loved every minute of it. While he respected his manager's decision to give him a rest, he was sad to be missing out on the start of yet another Premiership campaign.

When Cantona parted company with United, he left a huge hole to fill in attack. Alex Ferguson scoured the transfer market, both at home and abroad, and decided that Teddy Sheringham was the best bet to replace Cantona. Sheringham arrived for £3.5 million; it was a popular move with Gary, who had witnessed his qualities at first hand while on international duty. Neville saw the similarities between Sheringham and Cantona and knew that, as Sheringham got on well with United's England players, the new signing would settle in quickly.

Neville classed Sheringham as one of his toughest opponents and the former Spurs man had often asked Neville and his fellow fledglings about life at United. So when the offer came in from United, it was no surprise that Sheringham was keen to sign. Neville was also pleased because he always approves when the club buys British players, particularly ones who are proven at Premiership level. The fact that Sheringham was comfortable playing as a support striker, dropping slightly deeper behind a main striker, meant that he was a direct replacement for Cantona and so the team would not need to change its style. Some questioned the logic behind buying a player in the latter stages of his career, particularly one who was lacking in pace. But Neville, for one, was in full support of the new signing.

United continued their winning ways by beating Chelsea on penalties in the Charity Shield. Neville, did not play in the match, but was nonetheless pumped up for the game. It was a positive message to send out to all their Premiership rivals and the Charity Shield triumph meant that the players added to their medal collection. For Teddy Sheringham, it was exactly the reason he had signed for United – to give himself a better chance of winning the top honours.

The opening day of the Premiership campaign saw Gary rested again as brother Phil continued in the side for the match away to Tottenham. United ran out comfortable 2–0 winners. Gary tells a story in *For Club and Country* from the match at White Hart Lane: 'After Nicky Butt had given us the lead, the Gaffer told me to get stripped off because he wanted me to go on and seal it up at the back. I said, "I'm just going to the toilet." When I got back we had scored again and the Gaffer turned to me and said, "Get your top back on!" The other lads on the bench burst out laughing.'

Neville got his first start of the season when he replaced his brother Phil in the away game to Leicester. United ought to have won, but ended up drawing 0–0. They went on to win their next three league games and the defence was looking vastly improved from the previous season. Neville knew the defending had been an area for concern and was committed to making amends this season. Alex Ferguson had told the players that conceding forty-four goals in the Premiership the previous season had been unacceptable and it seems his words had already prompted better defensive displays.

The end of September was a poor patch for United, however. Draws against Bolton and Chelsea were disappointing and the 1–0 defeat against bitter rivals Leeds at Elland Road was particularly hard for Neville to take. But, as Gary identified, United suffered a more significant setback than the loss of three points that afternoon. The new United captain Roy Keane was stretchered from the field and his injury would have far more harmful ramifications than the defeat against Leeds. Deprived of Keane, who had a lengthy spell on the sidelines with a cruciate ligament injury ahead of him, United faced Juventus in their first Champions League group game of the season. The Italian side – a side with a renowned European pedigree – were the type of team that United needed to beat to gain more respect among the other top-flight European clubs.

But Neville knew that no player is bigger than the club and that life without Keane had to go on regardless. United were chasing success in a number of competitions and they had to stay focused. Ferguson had assembled a squad with many star players and he hoped that the club had the strength in depth to cope with setbacks such as this. Neville reminded himself of how the team had managed to progress despite the loss of Mark Hughes, Paul Ince and Andrei Kanchelskis and was full of confidence that United would still be a force to be reckoned with. Besides, there were some big games coming up.

The way Neville spoke about the upcoming matches for club and country against Juventus and Italy led to lavish praise from Peter Fitton in the *Sun*: 'In the best-informed football circles, Gary Neville is known quite simply as FEC. A short and convenient code once shrewdly applied in the cricket world to Mike Atherton and standing for Future England Captain. Yet this very composed, highly organised young man is already focused on a more immediate and demanding objective in his soccer life.' Fitton was referring to Neville's determination to triumph with both United and England.

First up for Neville was Juventus, United's opening fixture in a Champions League group that also contained FC Kosice and Feyenoord. Going a goal behind in the first minute was a less than ideal start but, led by the phenomenal Ryan Giggs, United stormed back to win 3–2. Giggs' performance was truly outstanding and Neville was awestruck by the brilliance of the Welshman, who he had grown up alongside at United. That night, Neville watched on as Giggs terrorised the Italian defenders and it was reassuring for Neville to see how defensively vulnerable the much-praised Italians looked. When Giggs runs at defenders, it is one of Neville's favourite sights in football and it was fitting that his goal was the one that clinched victory for United. Neville has always held Giggs in the highest esteem, calling the Welshman 'different class' and 'the best left-winger in the world'.

Neville then turned his attention to England's fight for automatic qualification to the 1998 World Cup. England and Italy were going toe-to-toe at the top of the qualifying group table and the showdown between the two sides in Rome, the final group match for both teams, became absolutely crucial. A draw would be sufficient for England to win the group and qualify automatically, but a win for Italy would put them top and force England into the playoffs to scrap for their World Cup chance. Although in the squad, Neville was left out of the starting line-up as Hoddle chose to play 3-5-2, with David Beckham on the right. It was a huge disappointment for Gary to miss out on such a massive occasion, especially after he had performed so well in recent England matches. When Glenn Hoddle told Neville 'I'm leaving you out', Gary understood the aerial advantage of playing Gareth Southgate ahead of him and that it was not a reflection on his performances. But it was still painful. It got worse when he arrived at the Olimpico stadium and saw the passion of both sets of supporters.

England battled heroically that night in Rome and gained the 0–0 scoreline that clinched automatic qualification. The image of Paul Ince in his bloody head bandage and the jubilant Ian Wright will always be remembered. Neville may have been an unused substitute, but was thrilled with the performances of the players involved. In fact, with the game reaching a nail-biting conclusion, Neville was grateful not to be brought on. As he explained in *For Club and Country*: 'Sometimes when you're a sub, you don't want to get on. 0–0 with ten minutes [to go] is such a time. If I went on and didn't adapt immediately to the pace of the game, it could have cost us a place in the World Cup finals.'

Both Neville brothers, Paul Scholes and Nicky Butt were all on the bench that night and only Butt got a piece of the action. Having played no part in the game, Gary felt a little detached from the jubilant celebrations come the final whistle and decided not to join in as the players ran to salute the England fans. He did not want to take the credit for the performance and so he left those who had played to soak up the applause. It was in no way a bitter, jealous reaction; rather one of a man who respects his team-mates and who did not want to encroach on their deserved celebrations. After all, England had secured automatic qualification for the World Cup and Neville would be able to experience the biggest stage of all.

After the game the England dressing-room was buzzing with excitement and Ian Wright cried tears of joy. Meanwhile, the Italians were putting a brave face on having to qualify through the playoffs. After the match, Neville knocked on the Italian dressing-room to ask Paolo Maldini to sign his shirt. Perhaps expecting a frosty reception, Neville was pleasantly surprised to be welcomed in by Maldini, who congratulated him on the result. It was a shock for Neville to see how calm and relaxed the Italians were, despite their disappointment. It left Gary thinking how different their mentality was, because no one would have been allowed into the England dressing-room after a game if the team had lost. It was also a nice moment for Gary, who had grown up admiring the consistent and effortless manner in which Maldini played the game.

*****

Back at United, the triumph over Juventus seemed to spark the team's league form into life. Barnsley were thrashed 7–0 at Old Trafford with a hat-trick from Andy Cole and Sheffield Wednesday received similar treatment, crashing to a 6–1 defeat. The goals were flowing, particularly from Solskjaer and Cole. Back-to-back wins over Feyenoord in the Champions League continued United's progress, but the second of those games against the Dutch side turned out to be a heated game full of unsavoury incidents. The 3–1 victory was achieved thanks to an excellent hat-trick from Andy Cole. Gary was in the midst of it all and it was one of the few times he has reacted furiously towards another player. Neville felt that Feyenoord's Argentine striker Julio Cruz deliberately elbowed him in the head and confronted him face-to-face.

The issue rumbled on when Neville celebrated United's third goal right in Cruz's face and the Argentine unforgivably spat in Neville face. When Cruz was substituted, Neville and a couple of his team-mates waved him off. The striker replied by telling the United players that he would see them in the tunnel. Cruz was not the only Feyenoord player to adopt an overly aggressive approach, yet somehow the referee did not produce any red cards. Denis Irwin suffered from a horrific challenge by Paul Bosvelt and the game was littered with nasty challenges. After the game, Alex Ferguson was so angry he urged his players not to swap shirts with the Feyenoord players.

Performances such as this increased Neville's belief that United were heading in the right direction with their displays in the competition. In *For Club and Country*, Neville said: 'We are now as confident as we've ever been in Champions League matches.' He saw the players had learned a lot from previous European campaigns.

But the champions were brought crashing down to earth at Highbury the following weekend, losing 3–2 to Arsenal in a game the players felt they should have won. Arsenal took a 2–0 lead, but United were dominating the game. Having pulled level through two Teddy Sheringham goals, Arsenal snatched the three points with a late David Platt header. Ferguson was furious that his side had not pushed on for a winner once they had equalised and it was an unhappy coach journey home. The manner in which Arsenal went toe-to-toe with United here was an early indication of the rivalry that was starting to emerge between the two clubs.

United's ability to bounce back has always been a major strength and so it was no surprise to see Wimbledon on the wrong end of a 5–2 scoreline in the following Premiership match. Goal-less at half-time, the game came to life in the second half as United's class shone through. It was not, though, one of Gary's better games, as he openly admits, but he sets such high standards for himself that any misplaced passes or bad decision-making really frustrates him. He even had a shot from distance that flew well wide – something Alex Ferguson commented on at half-time!

The quality performances continued. United overcame Blackburn 4–0 and then travelled to Anfield to face Liverpool. Two goals from Cole and a David Beckham free-kick were enough to secure a 3–1 win. Neville was typically bullish after the win. For him, there is no better away ground than Anfield to secure a win and he loves silencing Liverpool's supporters with a dominant performance. The form of the United's attacking players, who were in full flow, was mesmerising. With Giggs, Beckham, Scholes, Cole, Solskjaer and Sheringham all fit, Alex Ferguson had plenty of options with which to chase the title. Sheringham, in his first season at the club, was proving a shrewd buy and showing why both Jürgen Klinsmann and Alan Shearer rate him as the best strike partner they have ever played with.

A gutsy 1–0 victory at St James' Park owed much to the brilliance of Peter Schmeichel, who made superb saves from John Barnes and Stuart Pearce. Andy Cole grabbed the winner against his former club as United stole the three points, despite not playing at their best. After a 2–0 home win over Everton, United ended 1997 with a slip-up away to Coventry. But they were back with a bang in the New Year, as they humbled a Chelsea team that had received many plaudits during the season 5–3 in the FA Cup third round. Neville was thrilled with the team's fantastic display. The team went into the match with a game plan and it had worked perfectly. They had targeted Frank Leboeuf's weakness against the high ball and sought to send aerial passes in his direction. For Neville, it was one of the most enjoyable matches he has played in. The victory also served as a reminder to the critics who had been claiming that United were not valuing the FA Cup as a high priority.

During the campaign, Gary's best friend David Beckham proposed to Victoria Adams, then a member of the pop group The Spice Girls. The pair had been in the headlines ever since becoming an item. It was a very special moment for Neville, too. Beckham asked Gary to be his best man and Neville agreed immediately. Gary had seen the relationship from its earliest days. He was with Beckham when his best friend first saw Victoria on *Top of the Pops* and Beckham said to Neville at the time that she was the one he wanted to be with. Victoria and David soon met and found they were well-suited to one another. It had not been easy with the constant media spotlight on them, but eighteen months after they met, they were engaged and Gary would be by Beckham's side on the big day when the couple married at Luttrellstorm Castle in Dublin in July 1999.

Everyone at United knew the circumstances of the much-publicised relationship had been difficult and they were all thrilled for Beckham. But it was not long before the jokes began about Neville's role as best man. The players predicted that Gary would hold the stag night at Bury snooker club and they started taking bets on how long it would take before people fell asleep during Neville's speech. Neville himself was in a relationship with Hannah Thornley, the sister of his United team-mate Ben, and Hannah became a very important part of Gary's life. Phil talks of both brothers being in 'steady relationships' in their book. Phil would later marry his girlfriend Julie Killelea on 30 December 1999, on the eve of the new millennium.

Back on the pitch, the season was about to take a downward turn as United endured a rotten run of results. A solid win over Tottenham was followed by defeats away to Southampton (a feature of the United glory years) and at home to Leicester as well as a 1–1 draw against Bolton at Old Trafford. It all added up to one win in the last five Premiership games for Neville and his team-mates. This run of results left Gary reeling and in a bad mood for days. It was tough, but there was still plenty of time to make amends.

Things did not improve for Gary, though. He was rested for the draw with Barnsley at home in the FA Cup in a match he was desperate to play in, only appearing as a substitute and almost conceding a penalty. But an away win at Aston Villa in the Premiership ended a nightmare few weeks for United and extended their lead at the top to seven points over second-placed Liverpool. The win was followed by victories over Derby and Chelsea in their next two Premiership matches and, despite suffering badly with injuries, the team seemed to be producing their usual post-Christmas form.

But in between the matches against Derby and Chelsea, United went out of the FA Cup, losing their replay away to Barnsley 3–2. The dressing-room was devastated and Neville was furious to hear suggestions that, as United were chasing Premiership and Champions League glory, the FA Cup was not top of their list of priorities. The players were hurt by the claims; they had been determined to return to Wembley after having missed out on the final the previous year.

The injury picked up by Ryan Giggs in the Premiership match against Derby was a crushing blow for United. After Keane's injury away to Leeds earlier in the campaign, it was the second devastating piece of bad luck United had suffered during the season. With important matches ahead, the timing of Giggs' pulled hamstring was disastrous. As Neville knew, United did not have a replacement for Giggs down the left-wing – it was something that would prove costly.

United's reward for qualifying from their Champions League group was a quarter-final tie with AS Monaco. Neville felt the draw could have been worse for United. He remembered Monaco's performances against Newcastle the previous season and noted that Thierry Henry – with whom Gary would soon be more familiar – was the top scorer in the group stage. United would respect Monaco, but they would certainly not fear them.

The memory of the elimination against Dortmund was fresh in the players' minds and Neville hoped that the lessons of that two-legged tie had been learned. The players had now competed in Europe for a number of years and the team had the experience to make a big impact. The younger players, Neville included, had been involved in tournaments since their youth-team days at the age of sixteen and the key points of winning knockout tournaments should have been taken onboard.

The squad was perfectly capable of reaching the Champions League final, provided they did not make silly mistakes. But despite their strong start to the campaign, United's season was blighted by bad luck and it continued with Monaco's pitch in the Champions League. The Stade Louis II, built on top of an underground car park, took several United casualties, including the influential Peter Schmeichel. However, the 0–0 draw with the French side in the first leg of the quarter-finals of the competition was a solid result for United and it set the return game at Old Trafford up nicely. A win would take United into the semi-finals.

Schmeichel's absence, along with the injuries to Roy Keane and Ryan Giggs, meant that Gary was selected as captain for the Premiership match against Sheffield Wednesday. Commenting in *For Club and Country* on the moment when Brian Kidd told him the news he would be captain, Neville said: 'I didn't smile, I just nodded, but inside I was happy. To lead out United is a huge honour.' Sadly, Neville will not recall his first match as skipper too fondly as Sheffield Wednesday outplayed a below-par United to win 2–0. The team's performance was poor, but niggles from the Monaco match were certainly a hindrance to the side.

United simply could not shake off their poor form. Injuries were certainly one reason for the slump, but the available players should have been capable of better results. The team was still full of internationals and it is hard to understand United's goal-scoring problems with

David Beckham, Paul Scholes, Teddy Sheringham, Ole Gunnar Solskjaer and Andy Cole all on the field – even though they were carrying injuries. A draw with West Ham gave further encouragement to the chasing pack, particularly Arsenal, who had several games in hand on United, and the Gunners' visit to Old Trafford was the next fixture for Neville and his team-mates.

The Premiership game against Arsenal could not have arrived at a worse time for United. Confidence was low, the treatment room was overflowing and the Gunners were on a title surge. And all of these things were apparent when the two sides met – Arsenal ran out worthy 1–0 winners. Marc Overmars was the scorer and the defeat provided a huge dent to United's titles hopes. While Neville and his team-mates remained six points clear, Arsenal had three games in hand. Gary remained confident that a return to form would still ensure United retained the title, but time was running out and Arsenal were looking imperious.

The big games kept coming. The second leg of the Champions League quarter-final was United's next challenge but, despite a pain-killing injection pre-match, injury robbed Neville of the chance to help the team's cause. He started the game, but was forced off early through injury. An early Monaco goal from David Trezeguet had put United on the back foot and left them needing to score twice to progress. Solskjaer grabbed an equaliser early in the second half but, hard though they tried, the players could not force the crucial second goal and United were agonisingly eliminated from the Champions League on away goals.

Neville and his team-mates were devastated. The dressing-room was silent and the same emotions of losing out on the title against West Ham on the last day of the 1994–95 season were flooding through Gary's mind. It was such a bitter blow, as the players were starting to believe they could win the competition. Typically, Neville refused to accept that the team had just been unlucky. He knew there would be other chances for United, but he was fed up of hearing it. He wanted the team to prove themselves. The fact he was unable to be on the pitch for most of the second leg only added to his misery.

With Arsenal in sublime form, United had to start winning games to try to hold off the Gunners. A 2–0 victory over Wimbledon kept up the pressure and a 3–1 away win to Blackburn raised the spirits of the players, especially as Ferguson now had a fully fit squad again. Arsenal were keeping pace, though, with two wins of their own and the outcome of the title race was still in their hands. When United only managed a point at home to Liverpool, and Arsenal beat Newcastle, it put Arsenal firmly in control and the trophy was theirs to lose. The Gunners were playing fantastic football, but the frustration for United was that they were not put under enough pressure.

The next match, at home to Newcastle, was another disappointing afternoon. A 1–1 draw ended any realistic hopes of denying Arsenal their first Premiership trophy.

Ole Gunnar Solskjaer's desperate lunge to foul goal-bound Rob Lee in the closing stages may have earned the Norwegian a red card, but it kept United's slight hope of catching the Gunners alive. But although it was still mathematically possible, the United players knew that Arsenal would not throw it away. The last three games were more about pride than about catching Arsenal and United won all three of them, but it was too little too late. Had Neville and his team-mates pushed Arsenal to the last day of the season, the Gunners would have struggled, as they ended up losing their final three league games – though, admittedly, there was little incentive for their players. Neville had always maintained that if United could have kept up with Arsenal then the closing matches would have proved tricky for the Gunners, but it was not to be.

On 3 May, the Gunners secured the title after victory over Everton, and the United players had to accept that it was not their year. In fairness, Gary came out with dignified praise for Arsenal's efforts. The Gunners' run of results had been worthy of champions and everyone at United knew it. In *For Club and Country*, he said: 'It's a remarkable run, something I've never seen before, and fully deserves the Premiership title. I can only congratulate them.'

*****

Missing out on the title brought all kinds of uncertainty at Old Trafford. The last time United had missed out on the Premiership title, Alex Ferguson had sold several first-team players and re-built the side, so everyone waited anxiously to see what the United manager would do. History had shown that nobody was assured of a place at the club. Even Neville, who had enjoyed a solid campaign, admitted his fears over his future at the club. Ferguson had commented at the end of the season that a few players were not showing the desire for success that he expected of them, which put everyone on their toes.

Neville knew he would have to keep working on his game and adding new elements to his play. It is interesting to see how concerned he was regarding his future, considering he had already won so much silverware at United. It proves again how, at the biggest clubs in Europe – such as United – a player cannot afford to be off their game for long for fear of being replaced.

The feeling of ending the season empty-handed was an unfamiliar one for Neville. It was a season that made all the United players hungrier to win trophies and it was a wake-up call for any players who thought that silverware would just fall into their laps at the club. The players were burning with desire inside to prove the critics wrong. Little did those critics know that in a year's time they would be made to eat their words in the most spectacular of ways.

Chapter 4

World Cup '98 and the Treble

With qualification assured, England played a number of friendlies in the build-up to the 1998 World Cup as Hoddle sought to decide on his final twenty-two-man squad to travel to the tournament in France. Of the seven friendly matches, England lost only once – to Chile – and won three of the games. Both Nevilles were named in the thirty-man pre-World Cup squad for the last three friendlies before the final squad was announced. When it was, there was heartbreak for Phil. It was a painful time for the brothers. Even though Gary made the squad – being told by Hoddle that the decision to take him was 'one of the easy ones' – he was greatly saddened by Phil's exclusion.

Gary's own meeting with Hoddle was short and so he went straight back to his room to wait for Phil's news.

By this stage, though, he was already doubting whether Phil would make it and a bad feeling was building inside him. There was a moment during his meeting with Hoddle when the thought that Phil had not made the squad flashed through his mind and he hoped this was not the case. But his fears were confirmed when he heard Phil return to his room and slam the door rather than coming to speak to his brother. Gary knew what this meant. He went into Phil's room and found him in tears. This was one of the most torturous moments of Gary's international career, but at least he was there to comfort Phil in such a devastating moment. Phil's exclusion took all the happiness away from Gary's day – one that should have been one of the proudest of his career. But after learning that his brother had not made the squad, nothing else seemed so important for Gary.

Nicky Butt did not make the World Cup squad either (both returned to England) and it was very tough for Gary to say goodbye to his close friends and team-mates. When it finally sunk in he broke down in tears. He later joined up with fellow United players Scholes, Beckham and Sheringham as they attempted to come to terms with what had happened. All the emotions of the day served as another reminder of just how much professional footballers care about representing their country.

The next few weeks were emotionally gruelling for Gary as he had to adjust to Phil not being a part of the set-up and he was quite low on morale. It was the first time that Gary had been selected for something when

Phil had not. But there was certainly no satisfaction for the older Neville brother at the recent reversal of roles. Eventually Gary was able to put his disappointment to one side and started to focus on the tournament. Back home, it took time for Phil to re-adjust and the constant media questions did not help matters. Missing out on the World Cup had been a crushing blow, but he would bounce back.

Prior to the first match, Gary expressed his excitement about the tests that lay ahead of him. On 11 June, he wrote in his column: 'What I'm looking forward to most is playing against the best strikers in the world. If you are playing against the real top men, then you are so sharp mentally, right at the peak of your game.' The England players would need to be on top of their game if they wanted to progress in the tournament, but Neville believed that the team should fear nobody and that they had a strong chance of winning the World Cup.

The disappointments were not over for Gary, though, as he found himself left out of England's line-up for their first World Cup group match against Tunisia. He had hoped to be starting the game after playing in the recent friendly against Caen, but in the end Glenn Hoddle opted for Darren Anderton on the right-hand side of a 3-5-2 formation.

England got off to a winning start, as goals from Shearer and Scholes earned the team a 2–0 victory. It put England on top of the group and gave them a good platform for the two remaining group games against

Romania and Colombia. With so many top teams in the competition, it was important for the players to get into their stride early on. Winning the group would ensure that England avoided Argentina in the second round. Neville received a big boost when he was named in the starting line-up for the second group game against Romania for his World Cup debut. But the occasion did not faze him. Having already played at Euro '96, it helped him keep any nerves at bay. It was a disappointing night for England, though, as they lost 2–1 to a late Dan Petrescu goal and surrendered any hopes of claiming top spot in the group. A point against Colombia, however, would still be enough to seal qualification.

He kept his place for the Colombia match, which England won 2–0 thanks to a Darren Anderton goal and a trademark Beckham free-kick (David's first goal for England). But Argentina were looming large on the horizon and it was clear that if England were to triumph at France '98, they would have to do it the hard way. Neville, though, was upbeat about the team's chances. He respected the Argentine squad, which boasted Gabriel Batistuta and Ariel Ortega among others, but felt that England should not be afraid of anyone. It was a game Gary was really looking forward to.

The second-round match with Argentina will always be remembered as the night David Beckham was sent off for kicking out at Diego Simeone. However, it was also a game in which England showed real strength of character and togetherness to play about seventy minutes, including extra-time, with ten men. Michael Owen's pace caused the Argentine defence huge problems and the England defence frustrated Gabriel Batistuta and Claudio Lopez. Argentina took the lead through a Batistuta penalty and England's equaliser also came from the spot, as Shearer converted the penalty awarded following a foul on the lively eighteen-year-old Owen. Owen then produced a fantastic run and finish to put England ahead, before a cleverly worked free-kick allowed Javier Zanetti to equalise before half-time. Beckham's dismissal at the start of the second half changed everything as England were forced to sit back and defend for their lives. Late on, England thought they had won it, but Sol Campbell's header was ruled out. Extra-time could not produce a winner; it was down to the dreaded penalty shootout once again. Having been eliminated from their past two tournaments on penalties, England were praying it would not happen again.

As David Batty stepped up to take England's fifth penalty, he needed to score in order to keep England in the tournament. Neville was desperate for Batty to score, but he knew that he would then have to take the next England penalty – in sudden death. It was one of the most nerve-racking moments of his career as he watched alongside his team-mates. Batty's spot-kick was saved, though, and Gary had to pack his bags for home.

Neville recalls the shootout and the dismay at England's exit, saying, 'Glenn [Hoddle] asked me if I wanted the sixth penalty. There were better penalty-takers on the bench, but I looked around and accepted I was probably the next one in line. As David Batty walked up to take our fifth penalty, I knew that if David missed we were out and if he scored I was up next. I have never been so nervous. I started thinking how I would take my penalty. I decided just to put my head down and whack it, but I never got the chance to put my plan into action. David's penalty was saved and we were out.'

It was sickening. After the long build-up to the tournament and some excellent patches of football, the England players were once again heading home as under-achievers thanks to a penalty shootout defeat. The dressing-room was silent as the players reflected on their bad luck, but none of them blamed Beckham. Beckham would have a tough season ahead of him after all the headlines he had made at the World Cup, but he was able to come through it.

On the coach, Neville comforted a visibly distraught Beckham and reassured him that everything would be okay. Gary knew his best friend would get over it, but it was still a very emotional moment. Amid Beckham's sadness, the United midfielder revealed the news of Victoria's pregnancy to Neville, who pointed out that Beckham should be focused on this baby rather than the incident on the pitch. As Gary explained, this was a welcome reminder that there are more important things in life than football and it was a big help to Beckham that his best mate was on hand to support him.

But the disappointment hung over the nation and

Beckham quickly became a figure of hate among many club supporters. For Gary, the public's response was very different from the reaction to their elimination to Germany at Euro '96. The public were more critical this time round, but then, of course, England had progressed a lot further at Euro '96 than they had at the 1998 World Cup. Argentina were knocked out in the following round by Holland, but it was France who were the eventual champions, shocking Brazil 3–0 in the final.

*****

It would be fair to say that the 1998–99 season was the most remarkable of Neville's career to date – this season will forever go down in history as the campaign when Alex Ferguson's United side secured the Treble. Questions had been asked after the team surrendered the 1998 title to Arsenal the previous season, but United delivered the most clinical answers during the 1998–99 season as they scooped the unprecedented Treble: the Premiership, the FA Cup and, most impressively, the Champions League. Ferguson had always coveted the Champions League trophy and the players were equally pleased at their manager's fulfilment of a lifelong dream.

For Neville himself it was a dream season. In what was an incredible campaign, the Champions League final surpassed all else in Neville's career. The players simply would not give up and their team spirit was a crucial reason for all the success during the season. That night in Barcelona, United cemented their place in the upper echelons of European club football.

For a United fan who had shouted from the terraces in his youth at Old Trafford, it was that bit more special to achieve such dizzy heights with his boyhood team. United had been, and still is, a massive part of Gary's life and he had played in the team that brought home the Treble. It was a proud day in the Neville household as Gary and Phil brought home medals from three different competitions. Arsenal's faultless finish to the 1997–98 season had shown the football world that United's dominance could be challenged and it led to Alex Ferguson investing heavily in the transfer market. In came Dwight Yorke, a proven goalscorer for Aston Villa and a man whom Neville had encountered at close quarters in Premiership fixtures. Yorke arrived for a fee of £12.6 million and was expected to fire United to success. Teddy Sheringham had performed admirably, but at thirty-two he would struggle to carry the burden of United's heavy fixture list. So the manager decided he needed to add a fourth forward to compete for a place alongside Sheringham, Andy Cole and Ole Gunnar Solskjaer.

Jaap Stam also joined United that summer in a £10.75 million move from PSV Eindhoven. Relatively unknown to many, the towering Dutchman was an intimidating presence and seemed a logical replacement for Gary Pallister, who had retired at the end of the previous campaign. He brought height and power to the back four and the previous campaign had cried out for a figure like Stam to command the defence. Jesper Blomqvist completed the trio of new faces. The Swedish left-winger was primarily bought as cover for Ryan Giggs, who had been troubled by niggling hamstring injuries.

Reassuringly, in intense games with vital points on the line, Gary still found himself surrounded by the players he had grown up alongside. Neville and David Beckham, his best friend, had forged a superb understanding down the right flank, while Paul Scholes had blossomed into one of the most technically gifted footballers in the country. Gary's brother Phil was in contention for a first-team place, as was Nicky Butt, who struggled with the obstacle of the colossal Roy Keane occupying his deep-lying midfield berth. Ferguson had managed to blend the old with the new as effectively as he had done in 1995–96.

Yet for Gary and his team-mates, the season took time to get going. United began with a 3–0 defeat to Arsenal in the Charity Shield, a result that heaped more pressure on the club. Not only was it a loss, it was a heavy one. Arsenal dominated the contest, scoring through Marc Overmars (always a thorn in United's side), Christopher Wreh and Nicolas Anelka. It was David Beckham's return to action in England after his World Cup red card and the match also marked Roy Keane's return to the side after having missed the majority of the previous season. But it was the quality of the Arsenal display that stole the headlines.

United qualified for the group stages of the Champions League with a 2–0 aggregate win over Polish outfit LKS Lodz over two legs. However, the result may have come at the expense of early-season form as the team drew their first two games against Leicester and West Ham – it was hardly the form of title challengers. When United suffered another 3–0 defeat to Arsenal, this time at Highbury, they already found themselves slightly off the pace. But with new faces in the team, they were bound to take time to gel. In addition, a number of the players had featured in the World Cup in the summer and had then returned early to pre-season training to play in the Champions League qualifiers. It meant that some of the squad, including Neville, had enjoyed very limited time to recharge their batteries for the new season.

But their form would pick up. A series of convincing wins re-enforced United's title credentials and Neville found himself in a side making great progress in all competitions. The goals were starting to flow and the results showed the team were heading in the right direction. Charlton were conquered 4–1, Wimbledon overcome 5–1 – with five different scorers – and Everton soundly beaten 4–1.

The New Year brought even more ruthless goal-scoring performances. Dwight Yorke's first Manchester United hat-trick sunk Leicester 6–2 at Filbert Street, while Nottingham Forest suffered the acute embarrassment of an 8–1 drubbing, with Ole Gunnar

Above: Gary in a young Manchester United line-up containing several of his future fellow first-team stars of the Ferguson era.

Below: Gary shares the glory of the European Under-18 Championship victory over Turkey with Man Utd team-mates Chris Casper (now manager of Bury) and future stalwarts Paul Scholes and Nicky Butt in July 1993.

Devoted to his club, Neville epitomises for many the never-say-die spirit of Manchester United.

Above left and right: Neville, in pensive mood, lines up in front of home fans at Euro '96.

Below left: Seeking some divine intervention during the knock-out penalties against Argentina at France '98, while *below right*, marshalling the defence at Euro 2000.

Classic Gary Neville – fired-up, impassioned and making his presence felt across the pitch

The Nevilles are a talented sporting family. Gary shares a talent for cricket as well as football with his brother Phil, while their sister Tracey has played netball at international standard.

Above: Dwight Yorke, Andy Cole and a bloodied Gary Neville celebrate victory in the FA Cup final against Newcastle United in 1999, the year of their historic Treble.

Below: Sharing the spoils with team-mate Phil – this time, the 2003 Premiership: Gary's sixth, and the eighth time Man Utd has won it in the last fifteen years – testament to Gary's contribution.

Best man, room-mate, and team-mate down the right flank – one of Gary's closest friends is David Beckham; they've shared a lot of games and a lot of glory over the years.

Above: Own goal! Gary scores a belter but unfortunately it's past his own keeper as England scrape past Finland 2-1 in March 2001 in a World Cup qualifier.

Below: Triumph! Unalloyed joy at beating old rivals Germany by a massive 5-1 in Munich in September 2001 in their next World Cup qualifier.

Solskjaer netting four times in the last ten minutes. The forward line was firing on all cylinders and the signing of Yorke was starting to look like a very shrewd piece of business.

After Arsenal had clinched the title the previous season, Ferguson must have looked back at a handful of matches where United had been unable to break down determined defences and wished for another attacking option. This year, in Yorke, he had a player who could terrorise defences at any level, and Yorke's partnership and understanding with Andy Cole led to some exhilarating displays. On Yorke's arrival, many speculated that he was too similar a player to Cole and that they would not be able to play together, but Ferguson had got it spot on.

United's spirit carried them through a tricky FA Cup tie in late January against arch-rivals Liverpool. It was during this season that Neville, particularly, stoked the fire in the Manchester United-Liverpool rivalry. It is not a feud that needed any extra spice, as many explosive contests bear testament to, with unbelievable passion felt by fans for their own club and equally staggering hatred oozing against their rivals. On 23 January 1999, Neville wrote an article in the *Times* newspaper on the theme of this mutual dislike ahead of a game between the two teams the following day: 'You might think the intense dislike that the vast majority of Manchester United fans feel towards Liverpool would grow less when you become a professional footballer. Well, it doesn't. The feeling of the fans has got to be mirrored by the attitude of the players, as we represent them.'

Such is his dislike for Liverpool that his 'biggest thrill in football' comes from winning at Anfield. While he has nothing against the Liverpool players, he simply loathes the club and there is no sign of this ever changing. This particular contest was typical of United's season, as they came back from a goal down to equalise and then score a winner, with both goals coming in the closing moments. His open remarks that he could not stand Liverpool or anything to do with the place led to the chant from the United supporters 'Gary Neville, he's a red, he's a red, he's a red, Gary Neville, he's a red, he hates Scousers' to the tune of 'London Bridge is falling down'.

In a funny way, Neville's anti-Liverpool comments saw his popularity at Old Trafford reach new heights. He had always been a favourite with the United supporters due to his consistent performances and the fact that he was a local lad, one who had come through the youth ranks at the club. But his popularity soared when he addressed the United-Liverpool feud and the United fans appreciated the way that a player was echoing the feelings of the supporters.

Unfortunately, though, his feud with the people of Liverpool has led to several nasty moments. Firstly, after the Worthington Cup final defeat to Liverpool in 2003, Neville found his drive at home filled with bottles of Worthington beer. But much worse is the story of a gang of Liverpool fans seeing Neville stuck in traffic near Old Trafford and trying to overturn his car while he was inside. He has also received abusive letters in the post. While he has since tried to tone down his comments, he remains as determined as ever to beat Liverpool at every possible opportunity. An running joke in the United squad is that all the players refuse to sit next to Gary on the team coach on the way to play Liverpool at Anfield for fear of a brick coming through the window.

While it is certain that Neville's comments come as a result of his devotion to United, a few people – probably anti-United football fans – have suggested other reasons for his outspoken nature. For instance, one idea is that, because he is from Bury, he is not a 'proper' Mancunian and so Neville thinks he has to try harder to show his allegiance to Manchester United. But anyone who has followed Gary's career at Old Trafford knows that his love for the club is both genuine and unbreakable.

His background has always been an important part of Neville's character. Bury is his hometown and he has always stayed true to those roots. He has not sought celebrity status, but instead has remained very level-headed. Gary, Phil and Tracey rank among the most famous products of Bury. In a population of approximately just over 60,000, the Neville family has earned great respect in the town. Alongside Sir Robert Peel, Cherie Blair and Victoria Wood, the Nevilles are huge success stories from the town on the northern side of Greater Manchester.

He tries to help out locally as much as possible and, with his parents' involvement at Bury FC, he is often involved in projects at Gigg Lane. In the 2004–05 season, Gary lent his support to an initiative at Bury FC to fill their stadium for an upcoming home match against Grimsby Town. Neville helped promote the event, saying at the time: 'Friday is a great chance for people in the town to show they care for their local team, so hopefully they will turn up in droves and help celebrate the anniversary while bringing in much needed revenue.' He also gave an England shirt signed by himself for the day's raffle prize.

*****

In February 1999, England manager Glenn Hoddle was sacked by the FA. Hoddle had continued as manager after the World Cup, but lasted only four more matches. His England team had only achieved a defeat to Sweden and a draw with Bulgaria in the first two Euro 2000 qualifying games and, despite winning 3–0 against Luxembourg in the third match, the win over the Czech Republic in November 1998 proved his final game in charge. Comments Hoddle made about disabled people being punished for their sins in another life caused so much controversy that the FA felt that terminating the manager's contract was their only option.

Hoddle's spell in charge had certainly not been without incident. There were times when his explanations of decisions were far from satisfactory. The Nevilles encountered moments when they felt let down by Hoddle's approach and they were not alone; Beckham also felt the manager's communication skills could have been better. The reasons for certain substitutions went unexplained and Beckham was stunned to hear Hoddle questioning his commitment to play for England. On another occasion, the players' concerns over the team's tactics were ignored by the coaching staff, despite proposed requests from Neville, Tony Adams and a few other team members. England were subsequently outmaneuvered by Chile and it seemed the change of manager had come at the right moment.

There had been several problems during Hoddle's spell as England manager, but perhaps the biggest was that he was very much his own man and he found it frustrating when players did not possess the quality that he himself had shown during his playing career. Howard Wilkinson took temporary charge for a friendly defeat against France before the FA finally named Kevin Keegan as Hoddle's successor. The majority of the country felt he was the right candidate and Keegan, who was allowed to continue in charge at Fulham as part of the agreement, enthusiastically took the reins. Under immense pressure, victory over Poland in Keegan's first match as manager was followed by three straight draws, one of which came in a friendly. Although they remained unbeaten under

Keegan, England would go on to win only three of the first seven games and were forced into the playoffs in order to qualify for Euro 2000.

*****

Noticeably at United, in the series of changes made during the summer, the right-back spot was one position not up for consideration. Neville had even worn the captain's armband once during the previous campaign and his defensive qualities never went unnoticed by Ferguson, who knew he could rely on Gary for consistent performances.

On the field, United's Champions League progress was solid. The club had made improvements in the competition over the past few years and were getting closer to finally triumphing in Europe. Having initially been restricted by the limit of only three non-English players, United were now a force to be reckoned with. Neville had reached the semi-finals in 1996–97 when United had been eliminated by Borussia Dortmund and the previous year Monaco scored early in the second leg of the quarter-final and United were left with too much to do. The squad was determined to put things right in Europe during this campaign.

United were faced with a very tricky opening group with Barcelona, Bayern Munich and Brondby, but the level of opposition stirred some of United's most exhilarating European performances in their history.

Thrilling contests with Barcelona, home and away, saw two 3–3 draws as United showed they had the flair in attack to compete with any team in the world. Cole and Yorke were relishing the European competition and it was hard to believe that it was Yorke's first season of Champions League football. A draw in the last group game with Bayern saw both teams qualify for the quarter-finals, certainly in better form than had been the case the previous season. Inter Milan, the Italian powerhouse, were to be their opponents, but United could take positives from the fact that, for all their quality players, Inter had won very little in terms of prestigious trophies over the past few years. A brace of goals from Dwight Yorke in the 2–0 first leg win put United in the driving seat, with David Beckham supplying the cross on both occasions.

It was a showcase of just how dangerous Beckham could be if given space to deliver crosses into the penalty area. It was also the kind of performance from Beckham that made Neville determined to pass the ball to his best friend at every opportunity. Neville received some criticism for not having the confidence to send in more crosses himself, but the Inter match proved exactly why his first instinct was to seek out his best friend.

Neville's understanding with Beckham, forged through years of playing together down the right flank, was a big strength for United and opposition left-sided players often found the pair unstoppable. Neville always knew what Beckham was thinking and they were very much on the same wavelength. Even after spending so many years playing football at United at every level, Neville would look on in awe at the technique and accuracy of Beckham's crossing. For all that, playing alongside Beckham certainly improved Neville's own crossing.

A courageous 1–1 draw at the San Siro in the return leg put United into the semi-finals for the second time in three seasons, with Paul Scholes grabbing United's equaliser. It was a nervous night for United, but they were grateful that the dangerous Brazilian striker Ronaldo seemed uninterested all night long. The performance gave the team a lot of confidence going into the rest of the season, especially having proven themselves away from home in Europe.

Meanwhile, everything was falling into place for Neville and United on the domestic front. The team's Premiership form was steady and the FA Cup quarter-final replay against Chelsea was another case of Dwight Yorke proving well worth his price-tag. United triumphed 2–0 and set up a titanic clash with the previous season's Double winners Arsenal in the semi-finals. United's commitment to the FA Cup had been questioned, but the full-strength team Ferguson picked for the Chelsea game and the determined performances from the players showed that United were desperate to go all the way to Wembley.

United faced Italian opposition again in the semi-finals

of the Champions League in the form of Juventus, a team with a history against Manchester United and a more formidable outfit than Inter Milan. Juventus boasted quality players such as Alessandro Del Piero and Edgar Davids, both of whom knew what it took to win the competition. The winners would advance to a glamorous final in Barcelona to face the winners of the Bayern Munich-Dynamo Kiev tie. Juventus, experienced and wily, would provide the biggest test so far of the European pedigree of United's talented players. The first leg in Manchester ended in a disappointing 1–1 draw and it needed a late goal from Ryan Giggs to rescue the club's dreams of European glory. United had performed poorly and Juventus deserved to go back to Turin with a lead, but Giggs' goal meant that the tie was still very much alive. Neville noticed some tired legs in the Juventus team in the second half at Old Trafford and hoped the team could get into a position to exploit that.

Chasing trophies in different competitions, especially when one of them is the Champions League, can make consistency very difficult. Playing on Saturday, then Wednesday, then Saturday again can lead to tired performances, well below a player's best. United managed to overcome such a predicament and, despite a few draws, were unbeaten in their last twenty games. Ferguson successfully juggled his playing squad over this intense period and United's form was superb. Neville has always been full of admiration for the way in which the United manager sees things in the long term and so has not allowed his younger players to burn out from playing too many games. Even though Ferguson may have been risking his own job, he has taken good care of his players, ensuring that they get enough rest during the season to keep them fresh. Neville's boss has often insisted that there are simply too many fixtures in England and to combat this problem he tries to rotate the starting line-up from time to time. Gary never likes to miss United games, but he fully understands that his manager is thinking about the players' futures.

In the FA Cup semi-final at Villa Park, United faced Arsenal with a place in the showpiece final at stake. With United still chasing the Premiership title and Champions League glory, some people suggested that the FA Cup was fairly meaningless to the players in the circumstances. But Neville strongly disagreed, claiming that the FA Cup is a huge prize for any footballer and that everybody at the club was determined to win it. The rivalry between United and Arsenal had developed over the past few seasons and the Gunners had enjoyed the upper hand in four of the last five meetings between the clubs. This gave Neville and his team-mates an extra incentive to defeat Arsene Wenger's side.

Although he was positive about United's chances of the unique Treble, Neville and the rest of the squad were focused on Arsenal. It would have been easy to have had an eye on the upcoming Juventus game, but if anyone had doubted their commitment before the game, United's performance against Arsenal proved they were

100 per cent up for the match. Gary had been to a Wembley final twice with United and he knew which one he had enjoyed more. A cup final is a painful day for the losing team, but it is a phenomenal feeling to lift the trophy and indulge in a lap of honour. Having experienced the winning feeling at Wembley, Neville wanted to be back there every year.

Having required a replay to see off Chelsea in their quarter-final, United also went to a replay in the semi-final – and what a replay! After a closely contested 0–0 draw in the first game, the two teams returned to Villa Park to find a winner. Goals from David Beckham and Dennis Bergkamp left the game locked at 1–1 after ninety minutes, but this does not tell the full story. Roy Keane was sent off for a second bookable offence in the second half and Peter Schmeichel saved a Dennis Bergkamp penalty two minutes into second-half injury-time, sparing the blushes of Phil Neville. Extra-time saw more Arsenal pressure and more Schmeichel brilliance. Then, just as penalties seemed inevitable, up stepped substitute Ryan Giggs. Seizing on a loose pass from Patrick Vieira, Giggs took on Lee Dixon and Tony Adams, breezed past them, created space for a shot and hammered it into the roof of the net past David Seaman. Off came Giggs' shirt in celebration; indeed, one of the most memorable photos of the Treble-winning season will always be the exuberant celebration of Giggs as he whirled his shirt round and round above his head. United's spirit had taken them over the line yet again and the pitch invasion and mobbing of the players showed just how much it meant to United supporters.

Giggs' goal was worthy of winning any game and it required such a piece of individual brilliance to separate the two teams. Neville remembers the pressure that United had to handle and the joy at seeing Giggs' strike beat David Seaman. Just when he was bracing himself for penalties, Neville's prayers had been answered. It was an incredible night for everyone connected with Manchester United. Gary reflected on Giggs' match-winning goal in the *Times*, 'To do it when he did, to do it at that time, in a cup semi-final, when we had had a man sent off – that is what makes him a great player. You cannot teach that.' Giggs was the first youngster from the 1992 youth team to progress to the first team and Neville watched him in training with the same wonderment with which he had watched Eric Cantona. Just as with Cantona, Neville was amazed at how hard Giggs worked in training, despite the Welshman's obvious talent. Gary learned a lot about being a professional from observing the way that the likes of Giggs and Cantona approached their football.

The United victory at Villa Park was a highly significant moment for the players on their road to the Treble, not only because they had reached the FA Cup final but also because their belief had reached a peak. There was a feeling of invincibility within the squad that would dig the team out of several holes before the unprecedented Treble was achieved. Neville himself was on a high after the win over Arsenal and admits to having had trouble getting to sleep, such was the jubilation after the game. Gary and his team-mates were still cautious about celebrating before they had actually won anything, but it was a massive confidence boost to take into the crucial matches ahead.

Next up for United was the second leg of their Champions League semi-final, with the club hopeful of reaching the final in Barcelona. However, ten minutes into the second leg and Filippo Inzaghi had dented United's hopes with a quickfire brace. It was the worst possible start and would have been enough to derail most visiting sides. But this United team was brimming with belief and determination and even, perhaps, a sense of destiny. Roy Keane, an inspiration all night, led the fightback with a brave header, and further goals from Dwight Yorke and Andy Cole sealed a famous victory. That night in Turin against Juventus was as good a night as any player could wish for and it will always stay in Neville's memory. The whole experience was phenomenal, albeit immeasurably draining emotionally. The players had fought for every ball and their reward was a place in the showpiece final of the year. Besides the joy of reaching the final, the triumph over Juventus was equally significant: it was the first time United had conquered a team in the highest bracket of European football.

The journey home was one of the most upbeat of Neville's career, but the realisation that they had won nothing yet stopped the players from getting too carried away. Neville's biggest ever game awaited and the focus moved to making sure that United became 'Champions of Europe'. Despite his sheer joy at the team's achievement, the ecstatic feeling soon left Gary as he and his team-mates set about continuing their hunt for trophies. Alex Ferguson had also warned about complacency and hoped that there was a bigger celebration ahead for the club. He ensured the players knew they had won nothing yet and that simply getting to the final was not enough. United had to win it.

On a night of such joy for everyone connected to Manchester United, it was a tragedy that captain Roy Keane and Paul Scholes, two of the team's most important players, had picked up bookings, thus earning them a suspension for the final. It was the cruellest news for the pair; they would miss the most important night in the club's recent history. Both players tried to remain upbeat afterwards in the dressing-room, but Neville and everyone else at the club was devastated for them.

United still had a lot of work to do, but the momentum was with them. They still needed to wrap up the title, and Arsenal were hot on their heels. They reached the final day of the season knowing that a win at home to Tottenham would be enough to guarantee the Premiership title. It may have been a huge game, but there was not a trace of complacency in the team. Many of the players recalled the devastation they had experienced after missing out on the title on the last day of the season in

1995 and Neville, for one, was determined it would not happen again. Ferguson had told his players that day on the coach never to forget how bad they had felt; it was a pain that had stayed with Neville ever since.

But Neville and United did not let it happen again. Despite an early Les Ferdinand goal, United bounced back to win 2–1 through strikes from David Beckham and Andy Cole. Step one of the Treble had been completed and the team soaked up the atmosphere in a day of celebration at Old Trafford. After losing out to Arsenal the year before, the triumph was especially sweet for Gary and the club. It had been hard work, but United had overcome the title challenges of Arsenal, Chelsea and Leeds. While the Premiership crown was a major achievement, the wider significance of the triumph was that United kept up their momentum going into the two finals that still awaited them. If they had failed to clinch the title, it would have been tough for Gary and his team-mates to lift themselves from their misery.

The next task facing this pioneering team was the FA Cup final against Newcastle at Wembley. Prior to the game, Neville refused to underestimate United's opponents. He also hit back at suggestions that the FA Cup was not a trophy United desired as much as others. Having produced some superb performances in the competition, Neville had reason to ask what more the team could do to convince the public. For Gary, the FA Cup would never lose its appeal and he had his eyes on a third Double of the 1990s, something that would put an exclamation mark on what had already been a phenomenal decade for United.

Two extra-time goals from Alan Shearer had taken the Magpies to Wembley and they had looked useful on their way to the final, boasting experienced professionals like Shearer and Gary Speed. However, they were no match for United on the day. Even losing Roy Keane early to injury could not prevent a comfortable win through goals from Teddy Sheringham and Paul Scholes. Ferguson was so confident of victory that he left Jaap Stam and Dwight Yorke on the bench to keep them fresh for the Champions League final the following Wednesday. Though Neville and his team-mates enjoyed the celebrations, their minds were surely beginning to fast forward to Barcelona, and the final chapter of the Treble.

After a gruelling campaign, there was one last trophy for the exhausted players to fight for – the most prestigious of them all. Neville would not accept any excuses about United's packed fixture list, as the final would be all about determination and skill. In fairness, if a player cannot find the motivation for a Champions League final then he is in the wrong job. The journey to the stadium on the coach was very subdued as the magnitude of the match began to sink in. Even Ryan Giggs and Nicky Butt, usually full of laughter, were quiet.

The final in Barcelona will be remembered as the most famous night in the history of this generation of

United players. The achievement alone would have warranted such a status, as the competition features such a fantastic calibre of opposition. But the manner in which Neville and his colleagues captured the trophy – the last-gasp heroics – made it the most incredible night in English club football. Trailing to a Mario Basler free-kick, United toiled and forced their way back into the game. Yet they were still behind 1–0 with merely minutes to go. Then it happened. A half-clearance from a corner was crossed back in by Ryan Giggs and slotted home by substitute Teddy Sheringham. Having come so close, Bayern were shattered. Incredibly, rather than re-grouping, United hammered on the door again and forced another corner. Beckham whipped in a trademark delivery, Sheringham met it at the near post, flicked it on and Ole Gunnar Solskjaer, as natural a finisher as Old Trafford has ever witnessed, stabbed the ball home. United had come from nowhere to snatch the trophy from the Germans. It was fitting that Beckham had been the provider for both goals, as his tireless running had rallied United to make the final push.

The sheer focus and belief of the United team came to the fore during the closing moments of the final. The players simply refused to accept they had lost the game and displayed amazing spirit. With the vast majority of the nation behind them, the United players had sensed Bayern could still be beaten, even in the dying minutes. This season was the pinnacle for Neville, the moment of sporting glory for which he had worked so hard. The United players were Treble winners – and Neville was one of them.

The Champions League triumph was the biggest success of a stunning season. While the Premiership demands the champions to show great consistency across a thirty-eight-game campaign, the Champions League is a competition that pits the best sides in Europe against each other throughout. Clearly, there are some weaker sides in the tournament but, in beating sides like Inter Milan, Juventus and Bayern Munich, United had proved their European pedigree at last. Alex Ferguson knew the significance of conquering Europe, and it goes a long way to explaining his long-term obsession with winning the trophy. The Champions League was Neville's first taste of action in a Manchester United shirt and the competition will always hold special memories for him.

But part of Gary's character will never allow him to settle on what he has – there is always more to achieve. In this respect, his mentality is very similar to Roy Keane's. Gary's devotion to the club and also to his manager ensures there is no lack of desire when a new season begins – no matter what has been achieved during the previous campaign. Even in the aftermath of this phenomenal Treble success, Neville urged for caution amid the celebrations. He felt that United needed to do it all again to show that the club was serious about dominating in Europe. The obvious temptation for the United players was to relax and think that they had won everything now. But, in reality, there was no time to take things easy. How could they possibly ever eclipse this season? The team had played breathtaking football throughout the campaign, proved their mental strength in several backs-to-the-wall situations and displayed an outstanding level of consistency across three competitions.

The feeling – certainly if you listen to Keane – is that too many United players rested on their laurels after this success and thought they had made it to the top. It was an incredible season and it filled the players' trophy cabinets, but it did not immortalise them. It was just one season and the challenges would be there again at the start of the next one. Seemingly, some of the players approached the upcoming campaign as if they had already made their mark in football. But this should take nothing away from what had been an incredible season. To maintain the high level of performance and consistency to sweep teams aside in three competitions had been a phenomenal achievement. The spirit that was formed within the United dressing-room was evident every time the team played and Arsenal, despite having had a very good season themselves, finished it empty-handed. It is difficult to imagine any team replicating the history-making Treble in the near future, despite all the money spent at Chelsea.

The team had realised its full potential but, while the Premiership continued to be within United's grasp, this

Champions League success would prove the team's one taste of European glory. Alex Ferguson received a further reward for his achievements when he was knighted on 12 June 1999.

Chapter 5

Continued Dominance

Having won the Treble the previous season, it is somewhat understandable that Alex Ferguson – now Sir Alex – did not invest heavily in the transfer market during the summer. Peter Schmeichel's decision to leave United after the momentous campaign forced Ferguson to seek a replacement and he chose the Australian Mark Bosnich to fill the void left by the Dane's departure. Ferguson had signed Schmeichel in the summer of 1991 for just £550,000 and, in return, had received eight seasons of both loyal and excellent service. It would prove very difficult to find a replacement that could live up to the immense standards of the 'Great Dane'. He had made so many crucial saves throughout his career and had bailed the team out of so many holes that it was hard to imagine a United side without him.

Speaking prior to the 1999–2000 Premiership season, Neville emphasised that the United players were fully focused on the task ahead of them. He explained in his *Times* column in early August 1999: 'The achievements of last season seem a long way away now. The new season is here and you have got to put Barcelona and the rest of it to the back of your mind.' He rejected claims that United would be complacent after the glory of the previous season. He knew the other teams in the league would be even more motivated to beat United now that they were Treble winners. Memories of finishing seasons empty-handed in the past were always sufficient to keep Neville focused. Having enjoyed the winning feeling, Gary was not prepared to give an inch to United's opponents.

Controversially, United opted out of the FA Cup during the 1999–2000 season in order to play in the World Club Championship in Brazil. This decision was met with widespread criticism. There were claims that the club was destroying the beauty of England's main cup competition. Gary could not believe the public's negative response. He loved the FA Cup, but the World Club Championship was a chance to take on the best and represent the Premiership. United simply had to take part. The whole issue was blown out of all proportion as the public latched on to a chance to belittle United.

There were some calls for United to compete in both competitions, but Neville was adamant that this was not feasible. The injury to his pelvic bone, which was threatening to keep him out of the opening game of the new season, had been caused by the packed fixture list and adding more matches to the campaign would be impossible to manage. Sir Alex Ferguson gave Neville the rest he required to regain full fitness. In actual fact, Neville missed considerably more time than just the opening game of the season. He had already missed the Charity Shield against Arsenal, which United lost 2–1 despite leading through David Beckham's first-half goal, and could only sit and watch from the sidelines as the team began the season.

In his absence, United made a solid start to their Premiership campaign as they picked up nineteen points from a possible twenty-one. The attackers who had fired United towards the Treble were looking just as sharp and several teams left Old Trafford smarting from heavy defeats. Sheffield Wednesday were beaten 4–0 in United's first home game of the campaign, while Newcastle were hammered 5–1 as Andy Cole destroyed his former club with four goals.

The rivalry with Arsenal was still simmering. The FA Cup semi-final against the Gunners had been one of the most gripping games of the decade – or indeed the century – and Arsene Wenger's side were looking to add to their 1997–98 Premiership title. Neville, aware of the Gunners' good run of results against United, was determined to break the hold that Arsenal were starting to enjoy over them.

United were competing for trophies on all fronts. Having won the Champions League the previous year, they played in the European Super Cup against Lazio, winners of the UEFA Cup. Lazio beat United 1–0 on the night, but it was the first of many trophies the team competed for that season. A terrific contest at Anfield – one which the injured Neville would have savoured – ended 3–2 in United's favour and it marked the Premiership debuts of goalkeeper Massimo Taibi and left-back Mikael Silvestre – two players who would have contrasting fortunes at Old Trafford. Two Jamie Carragher own goals and an Andy Cole strike gave the watching Neville something to smile about.

The team's form was solid, with the odd blip along the way. A 5–0 thrashing against Chelsea at Stamford Bridge was a definite low point, as was a defeat against Tottenham, but a 100 per cent record at home in the Premiership through October and November put United in a good position. The Champions League was also going to plan for the club. Drawn with Marseille, Croatia Zagreb and Sturm Graz in the first group stage, United topped the pile with four wins, one draw and one defeat from the six matches. The second group stage provided a much sterner test, as United faced Fiorentina, Valencia and Bordeaux.

On the international scene, England awaited their opponent in the playoffs for a place at Euro 2000. The draw paired them with Scotland, with the two teams fighting it out for a chance to play in Holland and Belgium. Neville knew from their clash at Euro '96 that these would be very tough games, but he was pumped up to record another win over England's neighbour. He was, however, unable to line up against Scotland due to injury but, as he had predicted, England won the first leg 2–0 at Hampden Park. Keegan had Paul Scholes to thank as the United midfielder popped up with both goals. Neville was forced to watch on in the hope that the players would secure qualification. The second leg ought to have been relatively easy for England, playing at Wembley against weaker opposition and with a two-goal advantage, but Scotland dug in and a goal from Don Hutchison ensured a tense final few minutes. But, ultimately, it was too little too late from the brave Scots and England had booked their place at Euro 2000.

*****

United's Premiership form was excellent in the run-up to Christmas – a testing time for any title challenger. Ole Gunnar Solskjaer struck four times as United crushed Everton 5–1 at Old Trafford and then a special performance at Upton Park saw West Ham beaten 4–2 with Dwight Yorke and Ryan Giggs grabbing two goals each. This was United at their best, playing sweeping, attacking football and Neville could only look on in admiration as the goals continued to fly in. On Boxing Day, Bradford were the unfortunate visitors to Old Trafford and they left pointless after a 4–0 defeat. United left it late, though, with all four goals arriving in the last fifteen minutes.

Having expected to miss only the first match of the season, a serious groin injury kept Gary out for long periods of the campaign. The enforced absence was both frustrating and worrying for Neville. The longer he was out injured, the more he questioned whether he would get back into the team.

He did not return to Premiership action until 20 November and, initially, he struggled to regain form and fitness. His confidence was shattered during the World Club Championship in January as he made two terrible errors against Vasco da Gama, which handed the Brazilian side two opportunities the Brazilian striker Romario wasted no time in accepting. The mistakes were completely out of character for Neville – he prides himself on his consistency – and the pain of contributing to United's defeat caused him a lot of heartache. With his brother Phil producing solid form and proving a success in the vacated full-back role earlier in the season, it was one of the toughest patches of Gary's professional career and his confidence was totally shaken. It might seem as if he has always cruised along at United, but there have been difficult times, and this was one of them.

Despite their disappointing performances in Brazil during the championship, United continued to outclass their opponents in the Premiership. A draw with Arsenal was followed by three consecutive wins over Middlesbrough, Sheffield Wednesday and Coventry and Gary was enjoying being back in the first team again. The one sad consequence of his return was that Phil dropped back to the bench, even though he had done nothing wrong. A 3–0 defeat at St James' Park against Newcastle was a disappointment, but United had been reduced to ten men for the last twenty-five minutes after Roy Keane's dismissal and it was in this period that Newcastle scored two of their goals. Normal service was resumed in the team's next match as Leeds' young, title-chasing side were beaten 1–0, with Andy Cole striking early in the second half. It could have been a bigger margin of victory, but United failed to convert several chances, including one which Gary fired into the side-netting.

Neville's importance to Ferguson was highlighted again in the home match against Liverpool. When Michael Owen came on as a substitute for the last fifteen minutes of the game, Ferguson soon moved Gary from right-back into the centre of defence to contain the lively Owen and the Liverpool striker did not threaten thereafter.

In the second group stage of the Champions League, despite a 2–0 defeat in Florence against Fiorentina in the opening fixture, United recorded four consecutive wins and then a draw in the final game to ensure their qualification from the group in first place. This supposedly gave United the chance to play weaker opposition in the quarter-finals, in contrast to the troubles they had faced after finishing second the previous year. But the draw cruelly paired United with Real Madrid, who had finished second to Bayern Munich in their group. United limbered up for the European quarter-final with an absolute demolition of

West Ham in the Premiership. A Paul Scholes hat-trick inspired a 7–1 rout and sent out a message of intent to the Real Madrid players. Poor Craig Forrest in the West Ham goal must have been cursing his luck – he had been the Ipswich goalkeeper when United beat the Tractor Boys 9–0 in 1995.

Neville, now seemingly back to full match sharpness, and his team-mates travelled to Madrid full of hope and a 0–0 scoreline put United slightly in the driving seat. The team owed a lot to Mark Bosnich, who made a string of impressive stops, including one to thwart Steve McManaman, and Neville and his fellow defenders were able to withstand long spells of pressure from their Spanish opponents. It left United with the simple equation that any margin of victory in the second leg at home would be enough to put them into the semi-finals.

This was the season when it seemed as though Roy Keane would leave Old Trafford, with a number of big European clubs coveting his signature, such as Real Madrid and Juventus. But to everyone's relief, Keane agreed to remain at United. Everyone at the club knew how crucial it was to keep their captain at Old Trafford, no one more so than Gary, who announced that if Roy Keane was now earning five times more than him, he would have no complaints. Neville had grown up idolising Bryan Robson for his all-action midfield displays and he claimed that if he had been a child growing up in the late 1990s, Keane would definitely have been his hero. United's form in the two games before the return match in the Champions League displayed more explosive attacking and deadly finishing as the champions stayed on course to retain the Premiership trophy. Away to Middlesbrough, United struck four goals as they won 4–3 and Neville was involved in United's first as his long throw forced Paul Ince to head into the path of Ryan Giggs, who struck a shot past Mark Schwarzer in the Middlesbrough goal.

Sunderland were also hit for four as United won 4–0 at Old Trafford and Gary came close to grabbing a fifth. Things were looking good for Europe, and Neville and his team-mates were confident as they awaited Real Madrid, knowing that a victory would take them into the Champions League semi-finals. But, in hindsight, perhaps games such as the Sunderland match were too easy; United had simply cruised to victory. It made it more difficult for them to find top gear again for European games.

The second leg against Real Madrid ended in despair for United. Having felt well placed after a spirited draw in the Santiago Bernabeu stadium, United found themselves 3–0 down against their Spanish opponents and unable to stop their slick passing and movement. An own goal from Roy Keane in the first half put United under pressure and two well-taken goals from Raul put the tie beyond Neville and his team-mates. Despite a desperate late surge, when United scored twice through David Beckham and Paul Scholes, Real Madrid progressed to the semi-finals. It was the end of the dream for United. They would not successfully defend the Champions League trophy, but they could have no arguments about the class of Real Madrid, who produced some excellent football in both legs of the quarter-final and who went on to win the competition. It was a lesson in how to play ruthless attacking football for United, who had simply been outclassed by their Spanish opponents.

The Premiership was proving easier than ever for United as they maintained their high standards and their challengers could not sustain the form to keep up with the Red Devils. The team lost only three league games throughout the campaign and United's consistency was a feature of their displays on the path to retaining the title.

The title was clinched at The Dell, of all places, one of United's bogey grounds, after an emphatic 3–1 victory. While the players did not receive the trophy after the Southampton game, the celebrations began as another medal was added to Neville's ever-growing collection. With no FA Cup commitments, United's players were able to stay fresh towards the end of the season and this, no doubt, contributed to their excellent form. Even with the Premiership signed, sealed and delivered, the quality of United's play did not dip and they went on to win their final four games.

The final league table showed United's consistency throughout the campaign: they finished eighteen points ahead of second-placed Arsenal and twenty-two ahead of third-placed Leeds. It was clearly going to be as hard as ever to prize the trophy away from Old Trafford but, in all honesty, United had won the trophy without a fight. Neville collected his fourth Premiership-winners' medal, capping a happy return from the injury nightmare that had ruined much of his season. Parading around Old Trafford with his team-mates and the Premiership trophy was a feeling that would never grow old for Neville, or Sir Alex Ferguson for that matter. Gary enjoyed basking in the applause of the fans and knowing that he had played his part in yet another triumph for the club. His trophy cabinet was quickly running out of space.

*****

The next priority for Neville was competing for England at Euro 2000. Under their new manager, Kevin Keegan, England could take plenty of positives out of their pre-tournament friendlies, as they held Argentina and Brazil to draws and the players headed to Holland and Belgium full of confidence. The team had been drawn in Group A, with tricky opponents Germany, Portugal and Romania, but the mood in the England camp was upbeat. This time Gary and Phil were both included in the squad, so there was no heartbreak in the Neville family, at least at this stage.

Neville, playing in his third major international tournament at the age of twenty-five, was selected in the starting line-up for England's opening fixture against

Portugal. They made a dream start, going 2–0 ahead through goals from Paul Scholes and Steve McManaman, but sloppy defending allowed Portugal back into a game that should have been finished. Suddenly, the Portuguese players had brought the score level by half-time with goals from talisman Luis Figo and Joao Pinto. The second half was tighter, but it was Portugal who seized the initiative and Nuno Gomes arrived at the far post ahead of Tony Adams to slam home what proved to be the winner. England desperately sought an equaliser, but the luck was not with them on this night in Eindhoven.

Many sections of the media were critical of the defeat, despite the quality of some of England's play. Kevin Keegan was equally despondent, commenting: 'You go 2–0 up and you've got to fancy your chances of going on to win. We've not conceded many goals since I came into the job, but we got caught a couple of times ball-watching. It is not the result I wanted, but we will have to take it on the chin.' After such a flying start, the nation was extremely disappointed with the sloppiness of the performance. Terry Venables, the former England manager, was disappointed with Keegan's tactics of playing four in midfield against Portugal's five. He told the BBC website: 'I think in midfield if you've got four players and they've got five, you are going to find it tough. I felt we had to match them, otherwise they would always get that space.'

It was not the start Neville and England had hoped for,

but victories in their next two games would still secure qualification, after Germany and Romania drew 1–1 in the other game from Group A. England's fixture against Germany had become a must-win game and this added even greater significance to the contest, as England went out to avenge the shootout defeats of 1990 and 1996. For Neville, it was the first time he had faced Germany, after missing the semi-final of Euro 96.

It was a scrappy match, but an Alan Shearer header from a Beckham free-kick, along with some determined defending, was enough to earn England a crucial win and send Germany to the brink of elimination. It all meant that a draw against Romania would be enough for England to progress to the quarter-finals and the players had shown that the spirit was still alive within the team. But the match against Romania ended in disaster, as England, minutes from a quarter-final against Italy, conceded a late penalty to allow Romania to pip them to second place. A rollercoaster match was level at 2–2 (a Shearer penalty and a Michael Owen goal) and England seemed to be safe, but the late drama changed everything. The added pain for Gary was that it was Phil who gave away the penalty with a reckless challenge so near to the end of the game. Having missed out on the 1998 World Cup squad, this was Phil's first major tournament and it was a harsh turn of events. Ioan Ganea converted the eighty-ninth-minute spot-kick and England were sent home in the cruellest of circumstances. It was Alan Shearer's final game for

England, but it was not the way that he or England would have wanted to bow out.

*****

Having dominated the Premiership but failed in Europe, Neville was looking forward to putting his injury problems of 1999–2000 behind him and focusing on the new challenges ahead. The disappointment of Euro 2000 had been a bitter blow for both Neville brothers and the upcoming Premiership season represented a chance to put things right. Gary, having missed the beginning of the previous season with a groin injury, was fully fit for the start of the campaign and was eager to add to his four title medals.

Ferguson again saw little reason to tinker with such a successful squad during the summer and he certainly seemed happy with his defence. He did, though, try to address the ongoing difficulty of finding a suitable replacement for Peter Schmeichel. Several goalkeepers, including Mark Bosnich and the comical Massimo Taibi, had failed to live up to the Dane's legendary standards and so Ferguson turned to Fabien Barthez. Barthez, with a World Cup-winners' medal in 1998 to go with France's recent Euro 2000 triumph, had experience in pressure situations and was widely recognised as a quality goalkeeper. In Barthez, it seemed that Ferguson had finally found a worthy replacement for Schmeichel.

The Charity Shield, which is rarely a true indicator for

the season ahead, was far from memorable for United. Chelsea, equipped with their new £15 million signing Jimmy Floyd Hasselbaink, were the better side on the day and won 2–0 with goals from Hasselbaink himself and full-back Mario Melchiot. United's day was made worse by the sending-off of Roy Keane for a nasty challenge on Gustavo Poyet.

Nevertheless, Neville and his team-mates made a solid start to the Premiership season, winning at home to Newcastle on the opening day before a couple of disappointing away draws against Ipswich and West Ham. The draw at Upton Park, though, was a particularly poor result as United led 2–0 before two goals in the last four minutes rescued a point for West Ham. Questions were inevitably asked of United's defending. Bradford were the unfortunate side to face the backlash, as United hammered six goals past them at Old Trafford, with two goals apiece for Quinton Fortune and Teddy Sheringham.

With Jaap Stam and Ronny Johnsen both suffering from injury problems, Neville found himself occasionally switched into the centre of defence. This was nothing new for Gary; he had played there before for United and it is actually his preferred role. He arrived in the United youth team as a centre-half, but Brian Kidd and Eric Harrison felt his best chance of breaking into the first team was at right-back. Even years later, having won countless trophies at right-back, Neville still prefers playing in central defence. From centre-back, he can be more involved in the play while he sometimes feels isolated at right-back. Gary commented in his newspaper column in early October 1998: 'I still feel centre-back is my best position. I know some people have said I'm too small, but I can't accept that.' So when Sir Alex Ferguson turned to Neville with Stam and Johnsen injured, it was an opportunity Gary was thrilled about and, as one might expect, he did a good job.

After four wins and two draws from their opening six matches, United put in a couple of sloppy performances to drop points against their rivals. Chelsea, with new manager Claudio Ranieri, trailed 3–1 in the first half, but fought back to snatch a 3–3 draw at Old Trafford. This was followed by a poor display in the Champions League, losing 3–1 to PSV Eindhoven, and the dismal series of results was capped by a 1–0 defeat at Highbury against Arsenal. The match was a tight contest, but a quick Arsenal free-kick caught United napping. Thierry Henry surprised everyone with an audacious swivel and shot that looped over Barthez and into the net. It made talk of the title already being sealed for United seem absolute nonsense.

On 7 October, Kevin Keegan resigned as England manager. He had remained at the helm after Euro 2000 for a 1–1 draw with France in a friendly and he took charge of England's first qualifier for the World Cup in Japan and South Korea – against England's biggest rivals, Germany. After suffering the unusual pain of a defeat against England at Euro 2000, the Germans were out for revenge. In the rain, in the last-ever match at Wembley, a long-range Dietmar Hamann free-kick skidded off the wet surface and beat David Seaman in the England goal. It was a sorry performance from England and Hamann's strike proved the winner. After the game, Keegan shocked everyone by resigning. Like Venables and Hoddle before him, Keegan had brought together a talented squad, but just could not take them to the glory the nation craved.

It was a sad way for Neville to say farewell to Wembley – a ground that had brought him so much joy in his career. However, he later looked back on the last days at Wembley less favourably, especially having played internationals at various club grounds across the country. Neville called Wembley 'a tired old stadium with a tired old atmosphere'. The England players found that the supporters at other grounds around the country were much more passionate and that they enjoyed the atmosphere more than at Wembley. The team travelled around the country, playing at Old Trafford, Anfield, Pride Park, Villa Park and White Hart Lane, and loved it. Neville admitted to the *Sun*: 'It wouldn't bother me if we never went back there and I think that is the feeling in the England dressing-room. There was so much cynicism at Wembley and you felt that the fans would start booing you as soon as things started going badly.'

Defeat left England already trailing Germany in the group and set up a tough qualifying campaign. Peter Taylor, having impressed with the England Under-21 side, took temporary charge for a friendly against Italy that England lost 1–0 and it was Taylor who first awarded the captain's armband to David Beckham. However, with the added upheaval of finding a replacement for Keegan, along with some testing qualifiers, Neville and his international colleagues were left facing an uncertain future.

There were other factors that caused Gary to feel unhappy. It was at this time that he broke up with his girlfriend Hannah Thornley after a three-year relationship. News broke in October 2000 that the pair had split and Gary was said to be devastated. Insiders felt certain that he would follow in the footsteps of brother Phil and best friend David Beckham, both of whom were now married. But it was not to be. It was a difficult time for Gary as he tried to put his sadness to one side and focus on his career.

Meanwhile, in the Premiership, there were signs of a revival. In true United style, their recent setbacks only inspired Neville and his team-mates to improve their performances, and a solid 3–0 victory away to Leicester saw United back to winning ways. Another 3–0 win, this time against Leeds, and a 5–0 battering of Southampton sent out a warning sign to the other title challengers. Neville, continuing in the centre of defence, played an important part in that string of clean sheets.

The team's Champions League form had been less than impressive, though. Two wins from their first five matches put United's qualification in jeopardy after defeats against PSV and Anderlecht. Of the two wins, the victory over PSV in the return match at Old Trafford was probably the highlight of the group stage for United. It was after this match that journalist Nick Townsend in the *Independent* heaped praise on Neville and the way he had recovered from the difficult period after his two mistakes in Brazil. He wrote: 'It is the manner in which both the brothers have responded to being hauled through the critical wringer, standing defiant against the sneers with their sheer durability, which so commends them to Sir Alex Ferguson and a succession of England coaches.' Neville had certainly bounced back impressively and had returned to his best form. His performance against PSV at Old Trafford was particularly commanding and it gave United a solid base. A 1–0 win over Dynamo Kiev was enough to secure United's place in the second group stage, but it could all have ended in tears, as Kiev wasted a golden opportunity to grab an equaliser. Had Kiev picked up a point, United would have been dumped out of the Champions League at the first hurdle.

The second phase of the competition, now a second group stage, offered United a generous group as they were drawn alongside Panathinaikos, Sturm Graz and Valencia – all opponents whom United would have been confident of beating, though Valencia would have to be taken very seriously. It represented a very good opportunity for Neville and United to reach the latter stages of the competition.

The 18 November saw Neville face the Maine Road crowd as United took on Manchester City in the derby match. City, in their first season back in the Premiership after their painful exile as far as the third tier of English football, fought hard in what was a typically rough Manchester derby. But it was United who came away with the three points, winning 1–0 thanks to a David Beckham free-kick. Neville, once more at the heart of the action in the United defence, kept City's forwards at bay.

Two wins out of two in the Champions League gave United the desired start to the second group phase, but in the Premiership they suffered a rare defeat at Old Trafford. What made the defeat even harder to bear was that the 1–0 victors were a Liverpool side inspired by Steven Gerrard. The win came courtesy of a curling Danny Murphy free-kick that had been awarded for a handball by Neville, something that would only have deepened his frustration about the result. Neville and his fellow United players responded with an eleven-match unbeaten run in the Premiership that saw them pull away from their title rivals. It began with victories over Ipswich and Aston Villa and included several noteworthy performances. Another league win over Villa – 2–0 at Old Trafford – was the scene of a rare Neville goal as he scored from close range from a Roy Keane cross.

*****

The sudden departure of Kevin Keegan after the defeat against Germany at Wembley forced the FA to scour the country for a suitable replacement. But English candidates were limited and it was not long before the search was widened to include foreign managers. With other domestic bosses such as Sir Alex Ferguson and Arsene Wenger unlikely to be tempted, the FA sought out Swede Sven-Goran Eriksson to take charge of the national team. Eriksson's appointment received a mixed reaction – some pleased that a big name had been attracted to the post, others furious that England had chosen a foreign manager. For Neville and his international colleagues, the much-publicised pursuit of a new manager had been rather unsettling and a 0–0 draw away to Finland three days after the Germany match – under the temporary charge of Howard Wilkinson – suggested that the situation had affected the players.

When Eriksson finally agreed to take the England job in January 2001, it was a welcome end to the speculation. The team faced a tough task to qualify for the World Cup after collecting a solitary point from their first two group matches. After starting the match against Germany, Neville did not feature against Finland, and the appointment of Eriksson meant he would have to prove himself to a new manager once again – the fourth manager of his England career.

The Eriksson era would get off to a winning start, as the Venables, Hoddle and Keegan eras had done. Spain were the opponents in a friendly at Villa Park and England performed well to claim a 3–0 victory. Neville played against Spain and kept his place for the qualifiers against Finland and Albania in late March, both of which saw Eriksson's England pick up valuable wins.

However, back at Old Trafford, United's FA Cup hopes were shattered at the end of January as visitors West Ham picked up a 1–0 win through a Paolo Di Canio goal. Neville was impressed with the Hammers' performance, which was full of commitment and passion. It meant there would be no repeat of the Treble, but United's Premiership form was showing no signs of any kind of crisis. The team followed the cup exit with a match against second-placed Sunderland at the Stadium of Light. It was a tough match in which three players were sent off, but United emerged with the three points. After the game, Neville told BBC Five Live that he was pleased with the result. 'I don't think there's any place in the Premier League that we have it tougher than here, so for us to get a win tonight is a big relief for us. We're delighted to come away with a 1–0 victory.' He refused, though, to accept that it had been a dirty game, despite the red cards. 'First against second you're always going to expect tackles, but I don't think there was a bad tackle in the game. For three players to be sent off, it seemed a bit unnecessary.' Having recognised that 'people enjoy it when we get beat', Neville knew the importance of picking up the win.

After a victory over Everton at Old Trafford, Neville and United travelled to Stamford Bridge to face Chelsea.

United were arguably the better side, but the contest ended 1–1. Gary was disappointed not to pick up all three points, but he spoke positively about the performance after the game: 'I thought we passed it well. I thought the front two caused their back three a lot of problems. I think we were the better team and I think Chelsea found it difficult to live with us at times.' He also highlighted the fact that United had all their injured players coming back at the same time, strengthening their push for trophies.

Back-to-back draws with Valencia in the Champions League had consolidated United's position in the second phase of the competition, without the team producing their best football. Neville was particularly pleased with the point the team earned in Spain. A less-than-impressive draw against Panathinaikos and a win over Sturm Graz proved enough to ensure qualification, but Valencia won the group on goal difference. This proved significant, as the quarter-final draw paired United with the German powerhouse Bayern Munich and, had United won the group, they would have faced Arsenal, whom they would have been more confident of overcoming. At the very least, they would have known the Gunners' strengths and weaknesses.

But the most significant result of the unbeaten run was the crushing victory over Arsenal that shattered any hopes the Gunners might have had of making a title surge. Dwight Yorke struck a hat-trick as United triumphed 6–1 and the margin of victory was an indication of the gulf in class and consistency between the champions and the Gunners, their closest challengers. The eleven-match unbeaten run had begun after a defeat against Liverpool and it was at Anfield that the run came to an end. Liverpool were the better side on the day, with Steven Gerrard running the show once again. Gerrard opened the scoring and Robbie Fowler struck the second. Liverpool were also unlucky not to receive a penalty for a handball by Gary. The matches with Liverpool had been far from enjoyable for Neville or United this season.

The defeat to Liverpool was the worst possible way to prepare for the midweek Champions League quarter-final first leg against Bayern Munich and the players needed to make sure their season did not tail off. The first leg was decisive as Bayern came to Old Trafford and went away with a 1–0 win, making United's job for the return match a tough one. The two clubs will always be linked by that night in Barcelona in the Champions League final, but at the Theatre of Dreams it was Bayern's night. A couple of Premiership wins in between the two Champions League legs gave United more confidence for the trip to Germany, but the team were incapable of producing a rescue act this time around and put in a flat performance. They found themselves two goals behind at half-time and, despite Giggs striking just after the interval, Neville and his team-mates suffered quarter-final heartbreak for a second consecutive year in Europe.

Roy Keane was furious at the poor performances in Europe, which could be said to date back to the first group stage, and he made his feelings known publicly. The United skipper blasted the way the team had played, claiming: 'The players gave it their all tonight, but we are just not good enough and maybe it's time to move on. Maybe it's the end of the road for this team, although I'm not sure. It's no good winning the Premier League, we need to step up a level in Europe.' While United crashed out, rivals Leeds overcame Deportivo to move into the semi-finals, providing further agony for United, who would have loved to have been given Leeds' route to the final.

The gloss had been taken off the season for Neville. The Premiership may have been wrapped up comfortably, but the defeat to Bayern and a surprise FA Cup exit at home to West Ham had exposed some of United's failings. While for most clubs a league title would have represented a phenomenal achievement, expectations at United are higher and the players had fallen short of the standards demanded by both the manager and the fans. A half-hearted end of the season, with United losing their last three Premiership games, summed up the way the latter part of the campaign had gone. The players celebrated with the league trophy after the final home game against Derby (which was lost 1–0), but the Premiership crown was the bare minimum the club required and it was not the jubilant party the players would have liked.

On the bright side, the players had secured the title by ten points, ahead of runners-up Arsenal, even though they had not always performed at their best. But Neville knew the top clubs were measured on European success and, as far as the Champions League was concerned, this simply had not been United's year.

Chapter 6

Back and Forth with Arsenal

The 2001–02 season began with Neville and United searching for a fourth consecutive title armed with two new big-name signings. Ruud van Nistelrooy arrived from PSV Eindhoven for £19 million to lead the line and Juan Sebastian Veron was signed from Lazio for £28.1 million to add more class to the midfield. United began the season shakily. Having already lost the Charity Shield to Liverpool, they snatched a 3–2 win over Fulham through two Ruud van Nistelrooy goals and then picked up two away draws against Blackburn and Aston Villa. It was clear that United would not have things all their own way this season.

The middle of August marked the occasion of Neville's fiftieth cap for England. Holland were the opponents in a friendly at White Hart Lane. It was a special day for

Gary who took great pride in the landmark, despite the team's 2–0 loss. He had missed the friendly win over Mexico and the victory against Greece in the qualifying group, so he was desperate to be back in the side for the Holland game. The defeat was not the way Gary had hoped to celebrate his milestone, but it took none of the gloss off the achievement. It was a fine effort, particularly when you consider that he was only twenty-six at the time, and it paid testimony to his incredible consistency. The loss against the Dutch was Sven-Goran Eriksson's first as England manager.

Domestically, though, it was a testing time for Neville. He admitted he was at fault for the first goal in the Fulham game and he was dropped for the Blackburn game – the first time this had happened in his United career. This seemed to bring out the best in Gary and he was grateful to Ferguson for the way he handled the situation. Neville came off the bench against Blackburn and felt more comfortable playing at right-back again, as switching between there and centre-back seemed to have had a detrimental effect on his almost legendary consistency. While he had played in both roles many times, they require different mentalities and he found it tough to adapt and feel comfortable at having to play both positions.

The biggest drama of the early weeks, though, was the sudden departure of Jaap Stam from the club. The release of his autobiography, *Head to Head*, caused big problems for Stam as it contained unsustained allegations against Sir Alex Ferguson prior to his move to Old Trafford. Lazio bid £16.5 million for the Dutchman and his exit was sealed. Questions were asked as to whether Stam's exit was related to the book or if Ferguson had decided the Dutchman was simply past his best. Some other negative press surrounding the book regarded comments made against a few of his team-mates, including the Neville brothers. The book labelled the Nevilles as 'busy c***s', apparently a name used for them in the dressing-room, and Stam also targeted several other big names in football such as Michael Owen and Patrick Vieira. But his biggest mistake was the inclusion of allegations against Sir Alex Ferguson. Once Stam's claims hit the back pages, he was in hot water. Publicly Ferguson said: 'Jaap [himself] is a bit embarrassed by it all. He's very regretful now and he has some making up to do in the dressing-room.' However, in private, it seems the United manager dealt with the issue more severely. Stam was the latest big name at United to have a run-in with Sir Alex Ferguson and he would face the same fate as those before him, including Paul McGrath, Norman Whiteside and Paul Ince.

Gary did not take Stam's words against the Nevilles to heart, however. Like Stam, he felt it was the media who had blown the whole affair out of all proportion. The newspaper serialisation suggested that Stam had taken a dislike to the Neville brothers but, on closer inspection, it became clear that this was not the case at all. Whatever the reasoning behind the move, Stam had gone and Ferguson quickly found a replacement in the form of Laurent Blanc, who arrived on a free transfer. Blanc, an experienced and successful defender, was bought by Ferguson in a bid to bring extra know-how to the back-line.

The Germans were looming on the horizon for Neville as England prepared for the crucial showdown in Munich; it was a game they had to win to have any hope of wrestling top spot back from their opponents. Sven-Goran Eriksson was still settling into the manager's role and many feared for England's chances of gaining even a point. However, it turned out to be one of the most amazing nights of Neville's England career to date and a night that will take some beating. Few could have predicted the scenes that were about to unfold.

England went behind to any early Carston Janker goal, but rallied to lead 2–1 at half-time through goals from Michael Owen and Steven Gerrard. The way the players bounced back gave England huge belief and they ran Germany ragged in the second half. Owen struck twice more to grab a well-deserved hat-trick and then a pass from Beckham found Emile Heskey, who added a fifth. Germany, so often impenetrable for England, were thrashed 5–1 and England had produced their best performance for a number of years. Neville will always remember the ecstasy of the achievement and he was full of praise for the performance in his post-match interview. He claimed it was 'a great night for everybody in England'. The players had held their nerve on the big stage and their slick football had overcome the Germans' organisation and strength. With the pace and power of Michael Owen and Emile Heskey up front and the precision passing of Beckham, Scholes and Gerrard in midfield, England were able to pick holes in the German defence. Things certainly looked bright for the future and Neville added: 'The great thing about tonight is how young that team is.' Gary was one of the oldest outfield players for England, along with Beckham and Scholes, at just twenty-six years of age.

Eriksson was hailed as a saviour and the possibility of automatic qualification was suddenly the focus of all England supporters. Neville was cautious, though, pointing out that the brilliant result in Munich would count for nothing if the team slipped up in their last two games. England went on to beat Albania 2–0 in their penultimate group fixture to set up a thrilling last round of qualifying matches. Unbelievably, England's reversal of fortune had put them in the driving seat. If they got the same result or better than Germany from the final match, Neville and the other England players would top the group and go straight through to the World Cup in Japan and South Korea. It was scarcely conceivable when Eriksson took charge of the national team that Germany could be caught at the top of the table, but England were now buoyant.

The Premiership table was looking less rosy, though. With Blanc added to the defence, it was taking time for him to gel with Neville and the other defenders. A 4–3 defeat at St James' Park highlighted the fact that improvement was required, but Neville urged the critics to be patient. He knew that big performances would come soon and that the team would get back on track once they stopped making silly mistakes. On 29 September, United produced one of the most incredible displays in their history. White Hart Lane was the scene of the staggering match, as United trailed 3–0 at half-time but came back for a famous 5–3 win. It was a reminder of the immense quality in the Manchester United squad, but it also provided further evidence of bad defending.

Neville gained some respite from the criticism of the United defence in the form of the vital international against Greece. Interestingly, Neville was quick to call for the fans at Old Trafford not to boo Liverpool players (or any other England players) during the upcoming and decisive World Cup qualifier. But then his problem has always been with the club rather than the players themselves. He explained to the media: 'If any player gets booed at Old Trafford in a month's time I will be disgusted. If that happens to any players, not just Liverpool players, I'd be rather disappointed.'

The players had done brilliantly to turn things around in the group, but the importance of the match seemed to make the England side freeze on the big occasion. Greece stunned Old Trafford by taking the lead and it looked like being a frustrating afternoon for England. A shrewd substitution to bring on Teddy Sheringham instantly reaped its rewards, though, as Sheringham arrived to flick a Beckham free-kick into the net for the equaliser after only ten seconds on the field. But Neville and his fellow defenders seemed caught up in the celebrations of the goal because Greece scored again less than a minute later, leaving England's hopes hanging by a thread. The latest score in Germany was being monitored all round the stadium and Finland were doing England proud and holding Germany to a draw. One goal could be enough to clinch top spot. The game wore on, but England's attacking play lacked any fluidity. David Beckham played like a man possessed, covering every blade of grass and, in his role as England captain, drove his team forward. Greece kept conceding free-kicks in dangerous areas and Beckham had several attempts without finding the net.

Neville was beginning to despair and felt that horrible sinking feeling, but he and his team-mates battled on until the final whistle. There was one final chance. A dubious foul on Sheringham gave England a free-kick in perfect Beckham territory with literally seconds remaining. The skipper stepped up and whipped a stunning free-kick past the Greek goalkeeper Antonios Nikopolidis into the net. The stadium erupted and Beckham was mobbed by his grateful team-mates. The final whistle blew shortly afterwards – England had drawn. The players stayed on the pitch, waiting to hear confirmation of the final score in Germany's match. They did not have to wait long as word came through that Germany had drawn 0–0 and the party began for Neville and his team-mates. Though it was a special day for all involved in the England set-up, the day really belonged to Beckham. Alongside his heroic efforts in the 1999 Champions League final, this was the Beckham performance that Neville will remember most fondly. Neville knew the England players owed Beckham a lot for bailing them out against Greece, but he was not surprised that his best friend had once again taken a starring role in proceedings.

After the ecstasy of the Greece game, Neville faced turbulent times at Old Trafford as the team continued to leak goals. More poor errors revealed a fragility in the United defence – a 3–2 home defeat to Deportivo La Coruna in the first Champions League group stage displayed some comically bad lapses from defender Wes Brown and goalkeeper Fabien Barthez. This was followed by a 2–1 loss at home to Bolton. It resulted in one of the few times Neville experienced United's defensive ability being called into question. The confidence in the side had dropped and the supporters were growing restless.

A fortunate draw with Leeds at Old Trafford was another disappointment, especially against such bitter rivals. United needed an Ole Gunnar Solskjaer strike to earn a share of the points, but they had further chances to win the game in the closing moments and squandered them all. Unable to grab a winner, United left the field frustrated at dropping two more points. After the match,

Leeds manager David O'Leary had plenty of criticism to throw at the United side, drawing attention to the shaky defence and the limitations of playing a lone striker. Such comments did not sit well with Neville during what had been a difficult time for United and he had some home truths for O'Leary. Gary suggested that it was O'Leary who had looked edgy on the touchline and shrugged off the criticism. But O'Leary's comments did seem to have some basis. The goals had been flowing at times for United but, as future weeks would highlight, the performances were not totally convincing with one up front. For instance, in United's previous game, a 3–0 victory over Olympiakos in Europe, it took the introduction of Solskjaer as a second striker with less than twenty minutes remaining to break the deadlock at Old Trafford.

A painful defeat against Liverpool at Anfield brought more criticism as a fourth successive title seemed to be slipping out of reach. More defensive frailities had been exposed and many were questioning the wisdom of selling Jaap Stam to Lazio. Laurent Blanc was struggling to get to grips with Premiership football and it made the team look tentative defensively. Despite a home win over Leicester, a 3–1 defeat at Highbury put Arsenal in the driving seat as they produced some glorious attacking football. The large sums of money spent by Alex Ferguson did not seem to be producing the goods when it mattered. On a brighter note, United's performances in Europe had ensured qualification from the first group phase. Despite struggling against Deportivo, they beat Olympiakos twice and took four points from the two games against Lille to clinch second place. The second group stage of the Champions League saw United facing Bayern Munich, Nantes and Boavista and the draw presented Neville and his team-mates with a good chance of reaching the quarter-finals.

Problems reached a peak in the Premiership when United suffered a 3–0 home loss to Chelsea, followed by another home defeat, 1–0 against West Ham on 8 December. But this seemed to finally kick-start United's campaign. Derby were beaten 5–0, Southampton hammered 6–1 and Aston Villa turned over 3–2, despite having led 2–0. United won nine straight matches in all competitions after the West Ham defeat, but Arsenal still held the advantage.

Neville was delighted with this run of form, but he acknowledged there was a lot more work to be done. United had won five games in a row and were now looking much more impressive, but catching Arsenal was going to take an unbelievable effort and Neville acknowledged that United were 'walking a bit of a tightrope'. The Champions League was opening up nicely for United as they cruised through the group stages into the quarter-finals. Two draws with Bayern showed that the United players could still compete with the big clubs and three victories and a draw in the other four games clinched the group for United on goal difference.

January saw United travel to Southampton to face the team they had beaten 6–1 in the Premiership earlier in the season. Neville insisted, though, that the goal-fest at Old Trafford would have no bearing on the game. He was just grateful to be playing at the St Mary's Stadium rather than The Dell, where United had endured some horrendous afternoons in the 1990s. The crowd at The Dell used to sit very close to the pitch and it provided a very intimidating atmosphere. Neville explained to the media: 'The first four or five seasons in the first team for me, it was a bad ground for us to go to. We've turned it around a little bit with a couple of good results. They struggled a little bit at their new ground at the start of the season, but they've turned that round now and they've had a couple of great results against Chelsea and Liverpool. It's a big game for us.' The game went United's way on this occasion. Despite Southampton taking an early lead through James Beattie, United ran out 3–1 winners as the players enjoyed the more comfortable atmosphere of the new ground.

As the Champions League reached the knock-out stages, United were confident they could show their best form. The quarter-final draw paired United with Deportivo La Coruna again. Deportivo had beaten United twice in the first group stage and so Neville and his team-mates were all out for revenge. At La Riazor, United produced a fantastic performance to earn their first ever win on Spanish soil at the thirteenth attempt. David Beckham and Ruud van Nistelrooy were the scorers, but the night was marred by an injury to Roy Keane that derailed United's charge.

The team safely negotiated the second leg to reach the semi-finals and were then in sight of another European final. But once more, injury ruined the party at Old Trafford, as David Beckham picked up an injured foot from a poor challenge by Argentine Aldo Duscher. For Neville, the injury to his best friend was a sad aspect of what had otherwise been a famous night. Having played alongside Beckham for United since their days in Eric Harrison's youth team, he knew that it was rotten luck for his mate, a player whose fitness levels were always so high and for whom this was the first major injury of his career.

Roy Keane's hamstring injury in the first leg also put a dampener on United's achievements and the team's injury problems overshadowed their fantastic performances against Deportivo. It is easy to forget that Deportivo had beaten United home and away in the group stage, so United's dominant aggregate win was certainly praiseworthy. Neville could now look forward to a semi-final against Bayer Leverkusen, conquerors of Liverpool.

In the Premiership, United's form was impressive, but Arsenal were relentless in maintaining their position at the top of the table. Led by sublime performances from Thierry Henry, the Gunners were on an impressive run, aided by the fact that their challengers were unable to apply sufficient pressure at the top. United simply could not put together a good enough run of results. Away wins against West Ham, Leeds and Chelsea showed United's quality as they racked up twelve goals in the three matches. Finally the players seemed to have clicked into gear, but it was too little too late as the title seemed destined to head to North London.

Inevitably, attention quickly switched to the Champions League. Presented with Bayer Leverkusen as their Champions League semi-final opponents, Neville and his team-mates ought to have seized the opportunity to overcome weaker opponents. But a sloppy 2–2 draw in the first leg, in which United led twice, left United with a tough task in Germany and, while they had managed to recover against Juventus in 1999, Leverkusen clung on for a 1–1 draw in the second leg to qualify for the final on the away-goals rule. The first leg will always be remembered by Neville with disappointment as he broke the fifth metatarsal bone in his left foot; it was an injury that ended his season and crushed his hopes of playing in the 2002 World Cup in Japan and South Korea. It was a cruel injury at the worst possible time for Gary. Ironically, the injury was identical to the one suffered by David Beckham two weeks earlier against Deportivo.

The final, painful blow United suffered came when they surrendered their title to Arsenal after the Gunners won 1–0 at Old Trafford. In front of a crowd of 67,580, United laboured and Arsenal were able to celebrate their wonderful season at the home of their great rivals. Neville ended the season trophy-less and, worse still, injured for the World Cup. United's fourth-round exit from the FA Cup against Middlesbrough, combined with their shortcomings in the league and Champions League, left everyone at Old Trafford dismayed and desperate to redress the balance the following year. The players needed to be much more consistent if they were going to catch Arsenal next season.

Roy Keane was typically outspoken about the failures of the team, particularly in Europe, and suggested that the squad was not good enough, that perhaps the players were still living off the Treble success. Such a claim could never be levelled at Neville, but it was one of the first signs that this team's break-up was not far away. Keane, having missed the 1999 Champions League final, had more motivation than most and Ferguson had reminded the players that they owed Keane a Champions League final after the skipper's heroic efforts in the semi-final in Turin. For his part, Keane was starting to see his hopes of playing in a European final slipping away from him.

Looking back on the season, it was one of despair for Neville, but it only increased his desire to return to winning ways the following year. This was only the third time that Gary had not picked up any silverware during a season, but he recalled that in the past United had always bounced back from setbacks. When Blackburn won the title in 1994–95, United followed it up with the Double in 1995–96 and when Arsenal triumphed in 1997–98, United won the Treble the following year. Neville admitted that some of United's performances had been unacceptable and that 'we have to accept that we have loaded the guns for our critics with our inconsistencies'. The team may have dropped points against some of the lesser teams, but it was losing the big matches that hurt the most – especially the humbling at Anfield. This should not detract from some excellent displays, though, such as knocking Deportivo La Coruna out of Europe.

Arsenal had been more consistent and United had to accept that the Gunners deserved the title. While Neville was happy to praise the champions, he felt United had somewhat gifted the Premiership crown to the Londoners. It had been a rollercoaster season for Neville, both for club and country. The 5–1 victory in Germany and World Cup qualification against Greece will stay with him forever, but the injury was certainly a low point for him, particularly as he had been playing so well.

But Neville vowed that United's rivals should beware the backlash the following season as the wounded beast of Old Trafford would be seeking revenge. Sir Alex Ferguson had announced that he would be leaving at the end of the season, but a change of heart saw him remain at the helm for a few more cracks at winning the title. This, in a poor season, was a shining light of hope as the club avoided a hectic summer searching for a replacement. Neville and his team-mates had huge respect for Ferguson and loved working with him. Together, United would be seeking revenge when the new season began.

Having worked so hard to help England qualify, it was cruel on Neville that injury had denied him the chance to play on the biggest stage. He had played in the four friendlies since the Greece game as England won one, drew two and lost one, but the broken fifth metatarsal ended his World Cup dream. Neville himself claims he was feeling in the best form of his life at the time and it was a bitter blow for him to miss out on the tournament and also a number of Premiership matches. At first, he held out some hope of making the tournament, claiming that even a five or ten per cent chance was worth hanging on to, but it emerged that club doctors later decided he had no chance of recovering in time for the World Cup. Rather than delay the matter any further, Gary nobly announced that he would not be available for the squad and gave Sven-Goran Eriksson time to decide on his replacement. Being so passionate about representing his country, Neville was initially inconsolable about missing out, but he soon put things into perspective – he knew he would have other chances.

The players headed for Dubai to begin World Cup preparations just after the end of the Premiership season, much to Neville's disgust. Never afraid to voice his opinion, Gary questioned whether the international fixtures were ever arranged in the players' interests and felt it was all hindering England's chances of World Cup glory. Certainly, a few weeks of rest would have been preferable for the players and he criticised the FA for causing the Premiership season to finish so late.

Neville's international team-mates drew their two final warm-up games against South Korea and Cameroon. Although a lot of the matches had been friendlies, England went into the tournament with only one win from their last seven games. It was hardly ideal preparation, but all involved with the England side hoped that once the tournament began, the performances would improve. How Gary wished he could have been a part of the action. With his team-mates off training, Neville remained in England. He had opted to stay at home rather than go out to the tournament and, though he needed to spend time recovering from his injury, he was in a position to weigh up offers to be on television panels, analysing the World Cup games.

England arrived at the 2002 World Cup in Japan and South Korea carrying the burden of great expectations. It is debatable whether the team had a realistic chance of success as they were missing key players such as Steven Gerrard as well as Neville. In addition, captain David Beckham was involved in a race against time to be fit for the start of the tournament after his metatarsal injury against Deportivo La Coruna. It had been Beckham's dramatic, last-gasp free-kick against Greece that had propelled England directly into the tournament, avoiding the tension of the playoffs, and his fitness was the subject of endless speculation leading up to the tournament. England had produced some fantastic performances in qualification, most notably the 5–1 drubbing of Germany in Munich, which will live long in the memory of every England fan who witnessed it. Neville picked the emphatic win as one of the highs of his season. But doubts still remained over England's ability to turn it on in the pressure of a World Cup.

England's reward for automatic qualification was to be drawn in the 'Group of Death' alongside old foes Argentina, Sweden and Nigeria. It was a tough draw, but the England camp was quick to point out that all three were beatable. With Phil missing out on a place in the squad as well, there was the unusual occurrence of an absence of Nevilles in the group of players selected by manager Sven-Goran Eriksson. Gary put on a brave face about being unable to go to the World Cup, saying, 'People keep asking me if I am devastated but, because I have played in a World Cup before, I have managed to stay reasonably calm, although watching the tournament with my brother Phil, also at home, will not be easy. Disappointment in the Neville family will soon be replaced by anticipation when the World Cup matches loom.'

Gary also appeared enthusiastic about England's prospects of success at the World Cup. He identified England's pace as an important asset and hoped the team would use their speed, despite the high temperatures in Japan and South Korea. Neville also commented on the influence England manager Eriksson had had on the team, making the players prouder to play for their country than ever before and getting the maximum out of every squad member.

Neville might have been thousands of miles away from the action, but he was regularly in touch with David Beckham to hear updates from the squad. England drew their opening game against Sweden 1–1, despite leading through Sol Campbell's first-half header from a corner by Beckham, who had been passed fit to start. But in the second half, Sweden were vastly improved and England wasted possession. Niclas Alexandersson grabbed the equaliser, which happened to stem from a mistake by Danny Mills, Gary's deputy. How England would have welcomed Neville's presence as they tried to protect their lead and then, by the end, their point. But Neville had kind words for Mills, saying in his newspaper column on 5 June 2002: 'As a fellow right-back, I felt for Danny Mills after Sweden's equaliser, because from his chest down to the shot from Niclas Alexandersson was four or five seconds. That is enough time to run thirty or forty yards, so some of the players will regret not closing Alexandersson down.' The second half received a lot of criticism from the English media and there was certainly room for improvement, particularly as they faced Argentina next.

Tension filled the air as England squared off with Argentina, four years after their controversial second-round contest at France '98. Neville sat glued to the action, hoping England could settle the score. It proved to be David Beckham's night of redemption as England triumphed 1–0 thanks to their captain's first-half winner. When referee Pierluigi Collina awarded a dubious penalty for a foul on Michael Owen, Beckham placed the ball on the spot and fired England into the lead. His celebration and the reaction of his team-mates showed what a huge moment it was. He had finally brought closure to the incident in St Etienne in 1998 and nobody was happier for him than his best mate Neville.

Beckham explains in *My Side* that he got in touch with Neville immediately after the game: 'Gary's a team player. The perfect team player. He knew exactly what it meant to win a big game like Argentina. He'd have loved to have been a part of it. He wanted every bit of detail about the party that was going on in Japan.' It was touching that Beckham called Neville to share in the joyous celebration.

The ecstatic response generated by the victory meant that expectations were high for the final group match against Nigeria. In fact, the game was rather meaningless and was played with little enthusiasm by either team. Nigeria were already eliminated and England needed just a point to ensure qualification. Therefore, few can have been surprised by the 0–0 stalemate. Neville looked on contentedly as qualification was secured and a very winnable second-round contest against Denmark awaited England. The Danes, very familiar to the fans as they had so many English-based players, presented no great fears for England and the game was clinched more easily than anyone could have imagined. Rio Ferdinand opened the scoring before Owen and Emile Heskey got on the scoresheet to complete a 3–0 win.

Brazil, past World Cup masters, now stood between England and a semi-final place. The big sides were dropping like flies and the path to the final had opened up nicely for the England players. Beating Brazil would probably see England become the favourites to win the competition. The match was so big that schools were delaying exams so that pupils and staff could watch the game before entering examination rooms. As Neville and the nation watched on, everything seemed to be going to plan as England frustrated Brazil early on and a mistake by defender Lucio allowed Owen to dart through to give England the lead. But, on the day, Brazil had just a little too much magic. A slick move before half-time involved Ronaldinho whose run and pass found Rivaldo, who found the bottom corner of the net.

If Eriksson's men had reached half-time ahead, it could have been so different but, at 1–1, Brazil's confidence had been restored. The decisive moment proved to be a free-kick, out on Brazil's right touchline, roughly in line with the edge of the penalty area. Ronaldinho stepped up to swing the ball into the box, but his delivery floated agonisingly over David Seaman and dropped into the far corner of the goal. Although it is always hard to tell, especially with the quality in the Brazilian side, it seemed a fluke, as the ball was surely intended as a cross. Gary and all England fans across the world watched in dismay.

Ronaldinho quickly turned from hero to villain as his late challenge on Danny Mills earned him a straight red card. But even with a man advantage, England laboured and Eriksson's substitutions had little impact. Brazil looked comfortable, despite being down to ten men, and closed out the game to qualify for yet another semi-final. This was a team that had been in the previous two World Cup finals and who would go on to make it three. On this particular day in Shizuoka, such experience proved a key factor. Neville and England would have to wait another two years before they got a chance to put things right.

The disappointment for the England players was compounded when they had to watch on as South Korea, Turkey and Germany joined Brazil in the semi-finals. Indeed, this was the same Germany who had been outclassed 5–1 in September 2001, but they had re-built the team and their players have the knack of producing the goods on the biggest stage in the tightest situations. Perhaps England had not progressed far enough since that famous night in Munich.

Missing out on the World Cup meant Neville was even keener to get back to playing football than ever. Arsenal had used the summer to make a lot of arrogant predictions of future achievements, but Neville was not convinced. He still held the Arsenal team of 1998 in higher esteem than the current crop of Gunners and was not afraid to say so. That team had pushed United all the way in the Treble-winning year and had some fantastic players, like Marc Overmars and Tony Adams. Neville felt it had been a drop in United's standards recently rather than an improvement from the other Premiership sides that was responsible for Arsenal's title success.

*****

The Manchester United squad has always been very adept at coming back from setbacks – such as the 2001–02 title loss – and the 2002–03 season would prove no different. Once again, United recruited a big name in the summer of 2002 as Ferguson attempted to bolster the centre of defence, a position in which Laurent Blanc had been found wanting. The man he turned to was Rio Ferdinand, who arrived at United in a £30 million transfer from Leeds United after impressing at the 2002 World Cup in partnership with Sol Campbell. It was a signing Gary welcomed and he was delighted to hear the ambition in Ferdinand's voice at his first press conference. Ferdinand was a big-money buy but, at twenty-three, he still had plenty of years ahead of him at the club and Neville rated him as the best centre-half in England.

Writing in his *Times* column on 17 August, Gary gave insights into the feeling among the squad ahead of the new campaign: 'It is not often at Manchester United that we pose for our pre-season team photograph without at least one trophy. Once is bad enough and, for a club of this stature, it is unthinkable that it should happen two years running.' The previous season had shown that spending money did not guarantee silverware, so Neville was wary of complacency setting in. He had learned a lot from the disappointment of the previous season and was desperate to prove the critics wrong. However, he was ruled out of the start of the season as he continued his rehabilitation from his metatarsal injury. Having already missed the World Cup with the foot injury, his frustration continued as he had to sit out the start of the team's title quest when he would have loved to be out there playing.

As is often the United way, the team made a sluggish start to the new campaign and did not look like a club out to make amends. Two wins, two draws and two defeats from the first six games was not the response that Neville had predicted at the end of the previous season. Rio Ferdinand missed the first few games of the season through injury, but while he soon returned to action, captain Roy Keane was ruled out and so it was difficult for Sir Alex Ferguson to field a full-strength team. Keane was sent off against Sunderland on 30 August and, facing a three-match ban and in the midst of controversy over his autobiography, he opted to have a hip operation that kept him out until 22 December. His twenty-six-game spell on the sidelines proved to be a large factor in United trailing Arsenal at the top of the table by the time he returned.

Neville remained positive about United's below-par start, but he knew that results had to improve if the team wanted to challenge Arsenal. United had left it too late the previous season, and so it was imperative that the club kept pace with the Gunners. Many neutrals had taken great pleasure in seeing Arsenal pip United to the title in 2001–02 and Neville was more than aware that United's slump had brought joy to fans all over the country. The same people who had only recently been praising United were now calling Arsenal invincible. But all Neville and the rest of the squad could do was look ahead and put things right over the course of the season. Gary pointed out where United needed to improve. He felt it was crucial to put together a long unbeaten run to put pressure on Arsenal at the top of the table and for the players to play with more passion.

In all, Neville missed the first seven Premiership games before making an appearance as a substitute against Charlton. The manager had given Neville forty-five minutes of action in midweek versus Bayer Leverkusen to build up his match sharpness and he restored Neville to the starting line-up for the next Champions League game against Olympiakos, a selection that underlined his worth to the team. It was a huge relief for Gary to be back in the side. His five-month spell out injured had been tough and he had been forced to spend much of the summer on crutches. Initially his foot did not heal properly, he had to have another operation and the whole problem dragged on much longer than he had hoped. But Gary returned with a very positive attitude. He had put the injury behind him and was ready to aid the team's push towards Arsenal. He recalled that when he had last been out injured, it had taken a long time for him to regain match sharpness. So this time he made sure he was 100 per cent ready and, with the team playing well, there was no need for him to be rushed back.

He was also thrilled to return to the international scene and reclaim his place in the national side. England had to refocus their efforts on qualifying for Euro 2004 and, once again, the expectation was not only automatic qualification but a tournament triumph, too. The schedule began with England travelling to Slovakia for their first fixture. By now, Neville had regained full fitness and made it clear that he was ready to return. Speaking to the media, he said: 'I have no worries about whether I can perform on Saturday. If I had any doubts I wouldn't be here. I would have rung Mr Eriksson and told him. But if he had any doubts about me he wouldn't have picked me. I will be fit for two games in five days.'

Despite Danny Mills' decent performances, such was his popularity that most people were keen to welcome Neville back into the side. Mick Dennis, writing for the *Daily Mirror*, said: '[And] when the curse of the metatarsal kept Gary from going to the World Cup, it was evident how much we missed him. Danny Mills hindered Beckham instead of helping him. So we are appreciating Gary Neville at last.' In a genuine show of modesty prior to the Slovakia game, Neville turned down the chance of a testimonial at United. In fairness, he had no need for the money but, even so, he was thinking more of not wanting to take money from the United fans. This gesture paints an accurate picture of

Gary's character, highlighting how selfless and down to earth he is.

Neville was coy about whether he felt he deserved to dislodge stand-in Mills for the match in Bratislava against Slovakia, saying: 'Whether he did enough to keep me out is not down to me it's down to Sven-Goran Eriksson. I'm not the England manager. All I can do is try to impress him in training as every player will try to do.' But the public knew that Gary's know-how would give him the nod, provided that he was fully fit.

He also sent out a rallying cry for England to fulfil their potential. With a world-class core of players, Neville felt England had as good a chance as anyone of going all the way in Portugal. Obviously, there is no accounting for luck and injuries, but Gary saw Euro 2004 as a real opportunity for the national team to end its thirty-eight-year barren spell. Neville knew that this and the 2006 World Cup might be his last chances to win a major tournament for England.

The trip to Bratislava, Slovakia, will stay long in the memory for Neville. Assessing the experience, Neville wrote post-match in the *Times*: 'Bratislava is the one and only city where I have been woken by the sound of gunshots. Like the rest of my England team-mates, I was trying to get a good night's sleep ahead of our match against Slovakia when a few almighty bangs got me jumping out of bed.'

The match was scrappy, but the England players were able to come away with a precious 2–1 victory. Neville was angered by the scenes in the stadium as the behaviour of sections of the Slovakian crowd was disgraceful. Two fans were shot at and Ashley Cole and Emile Heskey were subjected to racist chants throughout the night. It frustrated Gary that these tasteless aspects of the game overshadowed what had been a very professional, crucial victory and that the media were always looking for a negative slant on any story regarding the national team. He, at least, was very proud of the character the side showed in Bratislava.

The pitch in Slovakia was also a great disappointment to Neville. It reminded him of Sunday league conditions and he could scarcely believe that these were actually the facilities for an international match. It made it very difficult to play passing football and Gary was quick to suggest that the football authorities should inspect the standard of playing surfaces. Considering the state of the pitch, it was to England's credit that they had the patience to wait for their openings.

The important win over Slovakia was followed by an embarrassing 2–2 draw against Macedonia at Southampton's St Mary's Stadium. Neville found himself playing in front of another big crowd for England as the team continued their tour of the country while Wembley was being rebuilt. He was still enjoying the atmosphere at these games and hoped the national team would continue to play at club grounds after the new Wembley's completion. England produced some quality patches of football, but conceded two sloppy goals. The second Macedonian goal was scored direct from a corner as the ball swung wickedly under David Seaman's bar and the goalkeeper failed to keep it out.

Home in the safety of Lancashire, the month of November was a mixed one for United and Neville. A series of solid victories in both the Premiership and the Champions League were only spoiled by a humbling 3–1 defeat to Manchester City in the derby. City's second goal was handed to them by an uncharacteristic error by Neville, who attempted to shepherd the ball out of play but allowed Shaun Goater, the City striker, to hook the ball away from him and drive a shot past Barthez. A mistake from such a diehard Red was thoroughly enjoyed by the crowd at Maine Road. As *The Rough Guide to Man Utd 2003–04 Season* explains, the City fans 'ensured Neville was cheered ironically for the rest of the game'.

Gary's devotion to United has always put him at odds with City fans. One famous incident occurred when Neville asked Noel Gallagher of Oasis to sign his guitar. Gallagher, being a diehard City supporter, could not resist the opportunity and wrote: 'Dear Gary, How many caps have you got for England! How many do you think you deserved? I'll tell you – f***in' none! Lots of love, Noel Gallagher M.C.F.C.' His error in the match against City haunted Neville. Making a crucial mistake in a Manchester derby was the stuff of Gary's nightmares, but he put the incident into context and made sure he did not let it affect his football. It was an occasion when his experience at the highest level was vital and Gary managed to move on from his disappointment at Maine Road.

Despite only dropping two more points that month (in a 1–1 draw away to West Ham), the United fans were beginning to show their discontent at the way in which the team was performing. The derby match was also significant for the first appearance of Peter Schmeichel, regarded by Neville as 'the greatest United player of the modern era', in the colours of Manchester City. This game, though, proved the turning point in United's season as Ferguson blasted his players after the defeat in a bid to revive the team's title challenge. Neville told *The People*: 'I've seen some outbursts from the manager, but that was as angry as I've ever seen him – and it was justified. The manager's not a liar. He said he might have to create a new team. That's not something I want to contemplate.' Ferguson's rant stirred his players into action and the results quickly improved. For Gary, the look of disappointment on his manager's face was not something he wanted to see again.

By the end of November, the critics were already sceptical about United's chances of winning trophies that season – something Neville struggled to understand. The team had only lost two of their past seventeen games as they went into their Champions League game with FC Basle, so it was hardly a major crisis at the club. But Arsenal were capitalising on every dropped point in the Premiership. December began in the best possible way for Neville – with a win at Anfield. A depleted United side profited from some extremely generous goalkeeping from Liverpool's Jerzy Dudek, who allowed a soft back header from Jamie Carragher to roll between his legs to present Diego Forlan with an absolute gift. Forlan added to that opener with his second after Sami Hyypia failed to clear and, while Hyypia made amends with a goal eight minutes from time, United hung on for a hard-fought win. Neville had a superb game, prospering in the heated atmosphere in what many regarded as his best performance of the campaign. It was the type of gutsy, backs-to-the-wall display that Neville has made a living out of and it was special for him to play so well at Anfield. While the luck had not fallen for United before, Dudek's mistake was a sign that the team's fortunes were about to change.

7 December was the day that United exacted some revenge on Arsenal, unleashing the pent-up frustration from the previous season. Without Keane, Ferdinand and Beckham, United still had enough determination and quality to win 2–0 through goals from Juan Veron and Paul Scholes. It was Gary's brother, Phil, who received all the accolades for his dominance in the deep-lying midfield role, outshining Patrick Vieira and Gilberto Silva. With this win, Neville and his team-mates pulled within three points of the Gunners and sent out a message of intent. By the end of January, United had reduced the gap to two points, picked up maximum points in the Champions League and had qualified for

the fifth round of the FA Cup and the Worthington Cup final. Despite a slow start, the team were still competing on all four fronts.

But England were still falling short of their best. After the criticism that followed the draw with Macedonia, the players had hoped to deliver a reminder of their quality against Australia, but were instead on the wrong end of a 3–1 scoreline. It was only a meaningless friendly at Upton Park, but the defeat was met with a barrage of negative comments. Harry Kewell terrorised England who, as planned, changed their entire XI at half-time. The second half featured a line-up of promising youngsters, including Wayne Rooney, Everton's teenage sensation. It was a night that Neville was keen to forget, but the fortunate element for England was that their qualifying group was very weak apart from Turkey and so the team would be able to bounce back.

Domestically, February saw Arsenal dump United out of the FA Cup – a match famous for the boot that Ferguson supposedly kicked, hitting Beckham on the forehead – and picked up a few sloppy Premiership draws. As Arsenal lengthened the gap at the top, more questions were being asked of United. The team's form in the Champions League, though, was very good, as United clinched their place in the quarter-finals. Neville, however, was still confident of catching Arsenal in the Premiership, especially as the two teams still had to face each other at Highbury. A consistent run-in would give the team a great chance of lifting the trophy and would increase the pressure on the Gunners. The United players had plenty of experience when it came to holding their nerve and Gary hoped this would give them the edge over the North London outfit.

The Worthington Cup, which United had often used as a chance to blood some youngsters, was taken far more seriously this season, not only by United, but also by a number of top clubs, including Liverpool, United's opponents in the final. It was not a memorable final for Neville and United – a special strike from Steven Gerrard and a late breakaway goal from Michael Owen sealed a 2–0 Liverpool triumph. Both sides had fielded strong line-ups and, from the disappointment etched on the United players' faces after the game, both sets of players had been desperate to lift the silverware.

But rather than derail United's season, the Worthington Cup final defeat proved the launching pad for their late assault on the Premiership. United's pursuit of Arsenal was flawless as they racked up wins over Aston Villa, Fulham and Liverpool. The players were able to relax in their last two Champions League second group stage matches – with Gary even scoring with a deflected shot against FC Basle at Old Trafford. United carried this excellent form into their European Cup quarter-final against Real Madrid, their European nemesis. The first leg, in the imposing Santiago Bernabeu stadium, was a night to forget for United as Madrid outclassed their opponents to triumph 3–1. United could take heart from the fact that Ruud van Nistelrooy, always dangerous, grabbed an away goal that gave his team a chance in the second leg. After van Nistelrooy's strike, Real looked wobbly for a spell and this also offered hope for the Old Trafford return match.

Neville was full of praise for the way Real Madrid had performed in the first leg. Writing in the *Times* on 10 April, he said: 'Sometimes you have to hold your hands up and praise the opposition and there were times in the first half on Tuesday night when Real Madrid were awesome.' But he insisted the tie was not over yet: 'I don't care how good they are, they are going to have big doubts if they are going in 1–0 down at half-time in the second leg with almost 70,000 Reds on their backs.' Gary hoped Real Madrid would pay the price for their attacking style of play and that United could target the gaps Madrid left as they pushed forward. The first leg had been embarrassing at times and Neville knew the United defence had to get closer to the Real forwards. The menace of Ruud van Nistelrooy had been the biggest highlight from the first leg and he seemed the player most likely to capitalize on any defensive mistakes from Real. Neville was unhappy to hear that United's stars had been ignored in all the discussions of Real's *galacticos* and he had a point. With players such as Keane, Scholes, Beckham, Giggs and van Nistelrooy, United had plenty of big-match players to rival the Madrid team. The biggest disappointment from the first leg for Gary was that the yellow card he received ruled him out of the second leg; he would miss the chance to make amends. Neville would have to watch on from the stands, hoping for a memorable night.

Bouncing back from the Real Madrid game, United took care of business in the Premiership in two huge games in the title run-in. First, in one of their best performances of the season, Manchester United pummelled Newcastle 6–2 in front of their own fans at St James' Park, with the attackers looking in irresistible form. Next, United travelled to Highbury for a momentous title showdown. The 2–2 draw did not really settle anything, but the reactions of the two teams and their managers told the whole story. Neville was only a substitute for the game, but he came on for the second game in succession and soaked up the jubilant post match atmosphere with his team-mates and the United supporters. Uncharacteristically, even Sir Alex Ferguson marched onto the Highbury turf to join in the celebrations. Arsenal, reduced to ten men with seven minutes remaining following the dismissal of Sol Campbell, walked off downcast and Arsene Wenger, their manager, seemed to feel the trophy slipping from his grasp.

The return leg of the Champions League quarter-final against Real Madrid saw a very special cameo from Ronaldo, as the Brazilian fired a hat-trick that crushed United's dreams. In front of a crowd of 66,708, it was another heroic United effort as they still managed to win the match 4–3, but they failed in their bid to overturn the deficit from the Bernabeu. It was far from a poor

United performance; the Reds gave everything in the quest for victory, but they ultimately came up short. Neville assessed the performance in his newspaper column a few days after the match, saying: 'There are things we could and should have done better, but not many teams will face up to Real Madrid and battle toe to toe with them. And let us not forget that we beat them on Wednesday night.' United took plenty of positives away from the match, especially the belief that they were not far from Real Madrid's level. Gary enjoyed seeing two offensively minded sides serve up a feast of football and the standing ovation given to Ronaldo when he was substituted showed that the United crowd had savoured a magnificent performance and a magnificent match.

While there were good points to take from the game, the players were devastated and it took a few days for the squad to re-focus their minds on the title race. With only the Premiership title left for United to play for, the players threw everything into the last three games of the season, away to Tottenham, at home to Charlton and away to Everton. When Arsenal dropped two points to a physical Bolton side earlier in the day, United knew that three wins from their last three games would seal the title and they made no mistake that afternoon at White Hart Lane. Initially denied by excellent goalkeeping from Kasey Keller, United had to wait until halfway through the second half before Paul Scholes broke the deadlock. Ruud van Nistelrooy added a second in the closing moments as the team gave themselves some breathing space ahead of Arsenal.

United continued the winning habit with a victory over Charlton at Old Trafford and, when Arsenal slipped to a home defeat against Leeds, the title victory was sealed for United. The final game for United at Everton was not the nervous last day they might have anticipated and, with the championship wrapped up, Neville and his team-mates marked the day they received the trophy with a 2–1 victory. For Neville, as United celebrated wildly at Goodison Park with the Premiership trophy, it marked the completion of an amazing comeback. Reflecting on the value of the 2002–03 title, Neville put this winners' medal on a par with his first title victory in 1996 and the medal from 1999, the year of the unique Treble. It had been a thrilling title race and the spirit displayed by the United players made the comeback as impressive as the one to overhaul Newcastle had been in 1996. Some of the squad were winning the Premiership for the first time and Neville enjoyed seeing the delighted faces of Ruud van Nistelrooy and Rio Ferdinand. At the same time, Sir Alex Ferguson and Ryan Giggs, for whom it was their eighth title, were just as jubilant as those for whom it was their first.

Sir Alex Ferguson viewed the 2002–03 title success as the team's greatest achievement and he looked on proudly as his players collected their medals and then the Premiership trophy. Indeed, one of the images of the season was of Roy Keane lifting aloft the Premiership trophy with all the United players and fans singing 'We've got our trophy back' and 'Champions'. It had been quite a comeback and Ferguson deserved great credit for rousing his players when their title hopes seemed to be slipping away. But as is typical of a character such as Neville, he was careful not get carried away amid the celebrations. In his column in early May, he explained: 'I know how short lived success can be. We are thrilled, but you end up with egg on your face if you overstate things.' However understated Gary was in front of the media, though, inside he was deliriously happy to have won the trophy back from Arsenal. He suggested that, in the past, United had taken winning the Premiership for granted, but vowed that the players would never do so again.

This trophy was a statement: it confirmed the team still had the desire and quality to overcome any domestic opponent and it was a fantastic way of hitting back at the critics. For Arsene Wenger and the Gunners, though, there was the pain of losing a title they thought they had wrapped up, a title race they had largely dominated. Like Kevin Keegan at Newcastle in 1995–96, Wenger's team had been ambushed in the closing stages of the season, although Arsenal never held the considerable double-figure lead that Newcastle United had. Arsenal went on to retain the FA Cup, beating Southampton 1–0, but it could not erase the devastation felt by the Gunners and their supporters. The Premiership trophy was the one they had really wanted.

Amid the many stars of the season, the biggest success was undoubtedly Dutch striker Ruud van Nistelrooy. With Dwight Yorke and Andy Cole having left the club, the goal-scoring responsibility lay in the hands of van Nistelrooy and he did not disappoint. Neville sang Ruud's praises throughout his prolific campaign and it was van Nistelrooy's goal surge that had pushed United towards Arsenal in the latter part of the season. He scored forty-four goals in the 2002–03 campaign, including twenty-five Premiership strikes and an incredible fourteen Champions League goals. It was an outstanding record and his efforts perhaps deserved more than just a Premiership-winners' medal.

Chapter 7

Paying the Penalty

The summer of 2003 will also be remembered for two big-money moves that would greatly influence the future of Neville and his United team-mates. Firstly, Roman Abramovich, the Russian billionaire, bought control of Chelsea Football Club in June – the first of several foreign takeovers in the Premiership. He made his agenda clear – he was willing to provide seemingly endless amounts of money, but he expected results and trophies. As many new faces started to arrive at the club, Chelsea suddenly moved into the bracket of serious title contenders. England-based players such as Glen Johnson and Joe Cole from West Ham, Juan Veron from Manchester United, Wayne Bridge from Southampton, Geremi from Middlesbrough and Damien Duff from Blackburn were all signed. In addition, Chelsea manager

Claudio Ranieri turned to the European market to sign Claude Makelele from Real Madrid, Hernan Crespo from Inter Milan and Adrian Mutu from Parma.

Meanwhile, at Old Trafford, the transfer of David Beckham to Real Madrid for £24.5 million was the biggest news to emerge in the summer of 2003. A devoted Manchester United supporter, Beckham eventually agreed terms with the Spanish giants and left United after over a decade of loyal service. His relationship with manager Sir Alex Ferguson had deteriorated to the point of no return and made Beckham's exit inevitable. For Neville, it was a crushing blow to lose such a valued friend and team-mate. The two had always linked up impressively down the right flank for United and they would miss this combination in the years ahead. Beckham's departure was very hard for Neville to come to terms with. Beckham, in his autobiography *My Side*, explains: 'Gary just didn't want to think it was true. I know we're best mates. I also know how much he loves Manchester United. He wouldn't ever have wanted me and the club not to be together.'

The two players, as close as brothers, had literally grown up together on and off the pitch. Their lives were dedicated to being professional footballers and the many hours spent in training and on away trips enabled them to form a real, lasting bond. The entire group of United players in that particular abundantly talented youth team were very close, something observed by Roy Keane in his autobiography *Keane*: 'They eat meals together, socialise with each other, have their own thing going. I recognise that the "kids" [Neville and co.] are the greatest strength the club possess, potentially. They form a core of United believers that other Premiership clubs don't necessarily have.' Eventually, Neville came to terms with the fact that his best friend was leaving the club. In the *Times* on 19 June, he revealed: 'There is a sadness in seeing him go. I have sat in the same seat on the team coach next to David Beckham for twelve years and it still feels weird to think that, from next season, that place will be filled by someone else.' But Neville understood that many exciting challenges awaited Beckham in Madrid. He would join a team packed with stars, but Gary was confident that his best mate could add to the club, not only with his set-pieces but also with his spirit and work-rate. Neville will always remember Beckham in the Champions League final when he was at the peak of his powers and he was excited about the adventures that lay ahead for his best friend.

While Beckham was heading out of Old Trafford, Sir Alex Ferguson was busy recruiting some young players who he hoped would have a bright future ahead of them. Ferguson had used Ole Gunnar Solskjaer on the right-wing towards the end of the previous season, but he felt he needed another option, too. Cristiano Ronaldo, the Portuguese winger, arrived from Sporting Lisbon for £12.24 million and he was seemingly hand-picked to replace Beckham on the right-wing. Brazilian Kleberson and Eric Djemba-Djemba of Cameroon both brought extra cover for the midfield. American international goalkeeper Tim Howard was perhaps the biggest new signing, providing stiff competition for Fabien Barthez and adding substance to the rumours that Ferguson had grown tired of Barthez's inconsistency.

Meanwhile, the defence remained unchanged. The summer was really rather disappointing for United in the transfer market, though. Ferguson had hoped to progress from the dramatic title victory by acquiring a couple of big-name signings. He was particularly interested in world-class midfielders, both defensive and attacking. Arsenal skipper Patrick Vieira was one name linked with the club, along with Leeds' Harry Kewell. But the biggest sadness was the failure to sign the mercurial Ronaldinho. It seems that United dwelt too long and Barcelona moved quickly to secure the Brazilian's signature.

The season began with United and Arsenal having reversed roles from the previous year. Now the Gunners were the side out for revenge, their pride hurt and the players' reputations at stake. United were the much-talked-about champions, but Chelsea had thrown their hat into the ring, too, with all their new faces. Neville acknowledged that 'Chelsea's threat is genuine' and knew they would push United and Arsenal all the way, but he did feel that their inexperience might be a problem. United and Arsenal squared off in the curtain-raising Community Shield, with Neville joined by a number of new faces. A close contest ended 1–1 and Tim Howard's impressive display in the shootout allowed United to hold their nerve for a 4–3 win on penalties. It was the positive start to the new campaign Neville and United had hoped for.

The team began the Premiership season positively too, racking up three wins from their first three games before a defeat against bogey team Southampton at St Mary's. Arsenal began effortlessly, taking thirteen from a possible fifteen points to begin their campaign. Arsenal's sixth game was a trip to Old Trafford, a game that saw all the tensions between the two clubs boil over in some rather unsavoury scenes. Gary missed the Charity Shield and the first two Premiership matches with a hamstring injury he had picked up in America against Celtic during a pre-season game, but returned with a bang, ready for the Arsenal clash.

This particular chapter of the United-Arsenal rivalry ended goal-less, but was certainly not without incident. Patrick Vieira was sent off in the final ten minutes of the game and United were awarded a ninety-first-minute penalty when Martin Keown was adjudged to have fouled Diego Forlan. Ruud van Nistelrooy's penalty cannoned back off the crossbar to the delight of the Arsenal players, some of whom crowded around the Dutchman, shoving and mocking him in a disgusting display of bad sportsmanship. It was a disappointing result for Neville and his team-mates as they missed the chance to gain ground on the Gunners.

Arsenal had actually performed very well, subduing United for long patches, but this seemed to have been lost in the controversial ending. The FA punished the behaviour of the Arsenal players after the game and handed out bans to Lauren (four matches), Keown (three matches), Parlour and Vieira (one match each). The club and the players received fines and, of the players that escaped bans, Ashley Cole was also fined. For United, Ryan Giggs and Cristiano Ronaldo were fined for their involvement in the chaos. United quickly regained their composure in their next few games, but questions were starting to be asked of this new-look side, complete with several inexperienced players who were playing in a title-chasing side for the first time.

*****

The draw for the qualifying groups for the 2006 World Cup took place in early December. The nation was expectant and many felt that the 2006 World Cup was the final chance for this group of players to win a major tournament. England were blessed with a straightforward qualifying group, which intriguingly included two other teams from the British Isles – Wales and Northern Ireland. Gary contacted Ryan Giggs straight after the draw was made, jokingly telling Giggs that England would thrash Wales and that he would mark the Welshman out of the game! Giggs promised to get one over on his United team-mate when the two teams met.

England were still in the midst of a tricky Euro 2004 qualifying campaign. A 2–0 win over Liechtenstein and a crucial 2–0 victory against Turkey revived England's hopes. For Neville, the Turkey game was important because it showed England could compete with the top European nations. The game will also be remembered as Wayne Rooney's first international start. Considering the high stakes and the immense pressure, he dealt with the big occasion with great maturity. Another 2–1 win over Slovakia and further victories against Macedonia and Liechtenstein set up a massive final group game with Turkey. Just as had been the case in their previous World Cup qualifying campaigns, England's recovery had given them the advantage. Neville and his colleagues needed just a point to win the group and ensure automatic qualification.

It was a huge match for the England players, but Neville could not wait to taste the white-hot atmosphere. Everything was set up for a big finale and, while some were fearing the trip, Neville was quick to reassure his team-mates. Having played in Istanbul before against Galatasaray in the Champions League, he spoke of the explosive atmosphere, which he deemed the best he had ever experienced. Furthermore, the England players had the chance to avoid the playoffs and clinch automatic qualification for Euro 2004. The nation was expectant and Neville knew the players simply had to deliver. Before the match he said, 'So there will be a lot more pressure on us this time and we have to accept that, go out there and do the job.'

The big off-the-field controversy surrounding the

game was the England players' threat to boycott the match in protest at the drugs ban imposed on team-mate Rio Ferdinand. Neville, seemingly at the forefront of the decision, explained the players' reasoning for wanting to pull out of the game. They felt Ferdinand had been pre-judged by the FA and had been found guilty without a trial. Gary explained in his *Times* column on 15 October: 'Yes, he missed a drugs test, but he deserved a hearing before people started passing sentence. Other players have missed drugs tests and not been banned, but Rio was punished even before he had the chance to explain himself. How is that not a pre-judgement?' Another aspect that had angered Neville and his team-mates was the lack of confidentiality. The FA denied they had leaked Ferdinand's name, but the manner in which they handled the issue made it obvious that something major had happened.

Gary also sought to defend himself and his colleagues against criticism for their boycott. The squad felt they had to show their support for Ferdinand and this was the opinion of not only the United players but of those from all clubs. The team thought long and hard and decided they had to stand up for their beliefs. Neville said: 'I have been lucky enough to play for twelve years for a club where, if you are in a tight spot, people will look after you as they would their own family. If that can happen at Manchester United, I would also like to believe it can be the same with England.' Looking back on the game, Neville could not understand why the media had been so critical of the players. In some quarters, he and his colleagues had been criticised for bringing disgrace to the England shirt with their actions, but Gary pointed to the show of unity among the players as something the nation should have been proud of. He added: 'In one of the most hostile football atmospheres in the world and against one of the best teams in Europe, we had to play under massive pressure because of the stand we took. We had the balls to see it through.'

David Beckham missed a penalty in an ill-tempered contest, but England played heroically to hold on for a 0–0 draw. The Turkish players took the setback extremely badly and some of their actions were disgraceful. Alpay, plying his trade for Aston Villa at the time, was one culprit and his behaviour – goading Beckham after his penalty miss – saw his Villa contract terminated. Graham Taylor, Villa manager at the time, and the rest of the Villa board took the decision that English football simply did not need characters like Alpay. In fairness, the termination of Alpay's contract suited both parties, as it had become impossible for the Turkish defender to continue plying his trade in England after the incident in Istanbul. On a more positive note, Neville claimed the players had bonded together over the turbulent few days and that the confidence within the side was as high as it had ever been. Team spirit had carried England through, despite the shameful provocation from the Turkish players. It was a night that made Gary immensely proud to be part of the national team.

Not everyone reflected negatively on the stand that the players took. Jonathan Northcroft, writing in the *Sunday Times*, preferred to take a more neutral stance. He claimed that while most people had pointed the finger at Neville as being the ringleader, there was actually a committee of senior players at the heart of the boycott idea. Northcroft added: 'There is no doubt, though, that as perhaps the most eloquent and forthright member of Sven-Goran Eriksson's squad, Neville played a prominent role.' Neville, already a Professional Footballers' Association (PFA) representative, has been heavily involved in negotiating with the FA throughout his time as an international footballer. He could undoubtedly do a job for the FA after he has retired but, with his clever thinking and passion, management seems a more likely option.

In the Premiership, United racked up important away wins against rivals Leeds and Liverpool, Neville's great foe. The Liverpool game was especially memorable for Neville because prior to the game he received the ultimate compliment from the then Liverpool manager Gerard Houllier. Houllier told the media: 'When we played United last season I was really impressed by Gary Neville's composure. In the past some of my team have lost their cool in tense situations such as happen in the big emotional games against United. That's why I was impressed by Gary Neville. He was always extremely focused no matter what happened.' Though this is all very true, most Liverpool supporters would have been furious to hear their manager's comments about a player who is loathed so much at Anfield. Clearly, Houllier viewed Neville very highly and felt his own players could learn a lot from the United right-back. All this praise came Neville's way despite some rather harsh comments Gary made regarding Liverpool that angered the Merseyside club's fans.

Just over a month after the momentous battle with Turkey in Istanbul, England took on Denmark in a friendly. In a very open and entertaining match considering it was a friendly, Neville and his colleagues found themselves on the wrong end of the 3–2 scoreline. The big story surrounding the game was another plotted boycott from the England players as they once again took on the Football Association, this time over its treatment of Leeds striker Alan Smith – who would later join Neville at United. Smith had been selected by Sven-Goran Eriksson but, as the striker had been arrested for throwing a plastic water bottle at a spectator, the FA decided to withdraw Smith from the squad. Reportedly at the centre of things again, Gary joined his team-mates in making their disapproval known and, though the game went ahead as planned, there were moments where it looked like negotiations had come to a standstill. His attitude in such situations has earned Gary the nicknames 'Red Nev' and 'Citizen Neville'.

*****

Solid home form was keeping United in the title race as the season reached the turn of the year and expectations were high: United historically produce their best football from January onwards. But this time the expected surge did not materialise. January and February saw the club drop precious points and slip further behind the rampant, fired-up Gunners who had still not been beaten. Home draws with Newcastle and Leeds, a home defeat against Middlesbrough and an embarrassing away loss to Wolves put United's defence under intense scrutiny. There was the odd chink of light, such as an entertaining 4–3 win away to Everton on 7 February with Ruud van Nistelrooy grabbing a late winner, but the trademark consistency of past United sides was missing and the defence was leaking too many sloppy goals.

The Everton game had been a big boost, but United still could not escape criticism as they were scolded for their celebrations following their winner. Neville dismissed the negative comments and told the *Manchester Evening News*: 'It is an over-reaction. We scored a goal in the last minute to win 4–3, so what do they want us to do, just walk back and say "Good goal boys"? Of course we're going to celebrate.' As the debate raged over defensive insecurities, ex-United and England defender Paul Parker put forward his suggestion for solving the defensive problems in the *Manchester Evening News*: 'We need stability and I think we have got to look at playing Gary Neville in the centre of defence. I'd put Gary in there alongside Mikael

Silvestre. He'll get people around him going. They fall into line and do what Gary says because nine times out of ten he is right.' Parker was not concerned about Neville's lack of height in the central defensive position because of the presence and the aggressive will to win he would bring to the role. The team was not having any trouble scoring goals; it was just the leaky defence that was the problem.

At least the FA Cup was proving a consolation as United saw off Northampton at Sixfields and set up a mouth-watering Manchester derby with City in the fifth round. While United triumphed 4–2, it was far from memorable for Neville, who was sent off for a headbutt on Steve McManaman before half-time. The BBC sport website claimed, 'Neville was guilty of diving as he was challenged in the area by Tarnat, and when he was confronted by a furious McManaman he clearly stuck his head into his former England colleague's face. It sparked a melee between players of both sides, which ended with Neville's dismissal.' But, writing in the *Times* after the game, Neville had his own take on the incident and sought to defend his actions: 'I was 100 per cent convinced at the time that I deserved a penalty. When I got up, three City players were rushing towards me. McManaman brushed his head against mine. When he came towards me again, I pushed my head forward in expectation of him doing the same.' He had no problems with the referee's decision because it had appeared to be an aggressive head-butt but, in reality, it was not. It was a momentary lapse from Gary, but it was only the second red card of his career in over 500 games and, as a defender at the highest level, that represented an excellent disciplinary record. The first dismissal, for a second bookable offence against Tottenham, is a moment of embarrassment and grave disappointment that he will never forget, especially as French winger David Ginola seemed to exaggerate the foul with an extravagant tumble.

March turned out to be just as cruel to United as February had been. Their league form continued to be shaky. Neville, serving his ban for the headbutt, had to watch from the sidelines as Manchester City hammered United 4–1 at the City of Manchester Stadium while their elimination from the Champions League was the most crushing blow of all. Five days prior to the fiasco against City, United had been shockingly dumped out of the competition by FC Porto, managed by Jose Mourinho, a man United would soon encounter at much closer quarters. Trailing 2–1 from the away leg, United led 1–0 at Old Trafford and appeared to be closing out the tie. But a late error from Tim Howard proved costly. He spilled a difficult free-kick from Benni McCarthy and Costinha was on hand to score the goal that sent Porto through. Neville described the elimination as 'a massive blow' and the players were stunned by their premature exit, with morale very low in the dressing-room. Porto went on to win the competition in a season of many surprises in Europe. United were beginning to make a habit of being knocked out by sides who then went on to lift the trophy.

The Champions League is always highly regarded at Old Trafford, arguably more coveted than the Premiership title and so this setback – and the nature of it – hit the players hard. As Neville explained in his *Times* column on 11 March: 'Manchester United have made a habit down the years of scoring late and dramatic goals, but now I know what it is like to be on the receiving end. It is a sickening feeling. The timing of FC Porto's goal was what made it such a cruel blow and we deserved better.' Gary was hurt by how badly United's season had gone off track. From a strong position, the team had fallen well behind Arsenal and had been dumped out of the Champions League. It was hard for Neville to accept, but he and the players had to try to repair the damage. He was quick to stress that United needed to step up a gear if they were going to push Arsenal for the title and he called for the team to show the courage and desire to put the Gunners under pressure again at the top of the table. Two upcoming matches against Arsenal in six days was the perfect opportunity for United to send out a clear message of intent; it also provided them with an opportunity to get their season back on track.

The first clash with Arsenal was a tightly contested draw, but United required a late Louis Saha goal to grab a point. Saha, signed during the January transfer window for just under £13 million, had contributed several goals, but he was powerless to stop United's inconsistency. The FA Cup semi-final between United and Arsenal was a huge contest for both clubs, particularly for United, for whom it represented a final chance to claim silverware from a troubled season. Neville was typically upbeat on the morning of the clash, writing in the *Times*: 'There is no point in trying to play down the importance [of this game] for United. Now we are out of the European Cup and too far behind in the league, it is the most important match of our season. It *is* our season.' The memories of the FA Cup semi-final replay between the two clubs in 1999 were fresh in Neville's mind and he knew that Arsenal would be out for revenge. The two teams had developed a fierce rivalry based primarily on respect and many expected another classic encounter. Gary knew it was unthinkable for United to finish a season empty-handed and he felt United had shown enough quality to worry Arsenal ahead of the semi-final.

The game proved as tight as many had anticipated, but Arsene Wenger made the decision to leave Thierry Henry on the bench to rest him ahead of upcoming Champions League games. This left Arsenal blunt in attack and gave United a psychological edge. United triumphed 1–0 on the day thanks to a Paul Scholes goal in the first half, conjured up by a combination of Neville and Ryan Giggs. The introduction of Henry and Jose Antonio Reyes with about half an hour remaining breathed life into Arsenal, but it was too little too late for the Gunners. Their chance of the Treble had disappeared and United had given themselves the chance to salvage something from their season. The FA Cup final against Millwall awaited them at the Millennium Stadium.

Almost as if the semi-final had warranted more effort than their league games, Neville and his team-mates finished the Premiership season with a series of poor displays. Defeats away to Portsmouth and Blackburn and the humiliation of a home loss to Liverpool were hardly the ideal preparation for the FA Cup final, but Gary added to his tally of United goals in the 1–0 home win over Leicester, striking the ball home after Cristiano Ronaldo's shot had been deflected to him. Neville, the match-winner on this occasion, was pleased with the win, but he still felt the team was failing to produce their best form. Unbelievably, Neville made it two goals in three games as he scored United's second in a 2–0 win over Charlton but, by this stage, any hope of getting close to Arsenal had been totally abandoned. The *Independent* echoed the shock of most spectators when describing Gary's goal: 'It was the manner in which the full-back picked up Saha's pass and sprinted into the area before driving a low shot into the right-hand corner of Kiely's net which would have really amazed onlookers.' Gary is certainly not known for his goal-scoring, but he has regularly expressed a desire to improve his finishing, as his roaming runs forward occasionally put him in shooting positions.

The FA Cup final was Neville and United's last chance of a trophy for 2003–04. In a rather one-sided game, despite Millwall's best efforts, United strolled to a 3–0 victory through goals from Cristiano Ronaldo and a brace from Ruud van Nistelrooy. The players produced the type of display Gary had called for in the build-up to the final and it was too much for Millwall to handle. Ronaldo's headed opening goal was crafted by Neville who delivered a perfect cross and Gary was full of praise for Ronaldo after the game, hailing his performance as 'particularly outstanding'. The players enjoyed the celebrations and, respectfully, the squad remembered Jimmy Davis, the young United striker who had died in a road accident in August. All the players wore a United shirt with 'Davis 36' on the back when they went forward to collect their medals and the FA Cup trophy. Neville told the BBC: 'Nine months ago, we had a team-mate. We still think about him and mention him regularly. Hopefully, what we did today will make Jimmy's parents smile for a moment.'

After all the criticism the players had faced, the FA Cup final win was a positive way for Neville and his team-mates to end a campaign in which their league form had been put to shame by Arsenal's outstanding unbeaten league season. As United spent the summer contemplating how to raise their game to the level set by Arsenal, a third title contender lay in wait, ready to strike.

*****

Neville could now look ahead to the upcoming European Championships. After missing the World Cup two years earlier, Gary was thankful to be part of the squad that travelled to Portugal. As was the case after qualification for the 2002 World Cup, England went through the motions in their warm-up friendlies. Two draws and two defeats did not show a squad in the best of form, but a 6–1 win over Iceland was a good boost just over a week before the tournament began. Having missed the 2002 World Cup, Neville was as determined as ever for England to make a big impression in Portugal. Placed in a group with Euro 2000 winners France, Switzerland and Croatia, England had once again received a tricky draw in a major tournament.

The opening fixture against France saw a heart-breaking defeat, despite a superb team performance. With Rio Ferdinand out due to his drugs ban and Sol Campbell struggling with injury, Eriksson turned to Ledley King to play in the centre of defence and contend with the threat of Thierry Henry. Frank Lampard put England ahead, heading home from a free-kick, and France were struggling to impose themselves. Things started to look even better when Mikael Silvestre fouled Wayne Rooney in the area and the referee pointed to the spot, but David Beckham's penalty was saved by Fabien Barthez. This proved to be the turning point. Let off the hook, France fought back and Zinedine Zidane equalised with a free-kick. As England fans began to accept that a draw would still be a good result for the team, the unthinkable happened. A backpass from Steven Gerrard fell slightly short and Henry's lightening pace ensured he arrived at the ball ahead of the onrushing England goalkeeper David James. As Henry went past James, the keeper had committed to the challenge and brought the forward down. Penalty. Zidane calmly slotted it home and England had been robbed of what should have been three points.

Such a heartbreaking defeat could have derailed England's challenge. Leading 1–0 in the closing stages, even a point would have been a disappointment, but to actually lose the game was a very bitter pill to swallow. Neville, though, took plenty of positives from the display. Speaking to the media, he said: 'It was a brilliant game until two minutes to go and it all went wrong for us. I don't think we could have done much more. Sometimes football kicks you in the teeth and that's what happened.' Gary also conceded that considering the quality of opposition, England could reflect on matching one of the very best international sides for almost ninety minutes: 'People expected France to beat us anyway to be honest, so we were in a position that many people thought we'd never be in. It was a great performance, one of the best performances you could wish for. It just went against us.'

To their credit, England bounced back superbly. Switzerland were beaten 3–0 with Neville's excellent work down the right-hand side crafting the third goal. The result put England back on track and kept their qualification hopes very much alive. Speaking after the Switzerland game, Neville was delighted to have got through the testing challenge of playing in such high temperatures with a victory. He told the press that the result was perfect, but that the heat remained a major concern: 'It was forty degrees pitchside, you were basically stopping for a drink every two minutes during training, your blisters were getting worse and I wore moulded studs for the first time in a game in twelve years on Thursday because the pitch was rock hard. We got through it and we got the result.'

Assessing the tournament as a whole, Neville observed that the 5.00 p.m. games had offered a lower standard of football than the 7.45 p.m. games due to the heat. The 7.45 p.m. games had been quicker and teams seemed to have more energy, allowing for better passing and movement. England's end-to-end, all-action style was certainly not suited to the high temperatures and Neville found it tough at times to deal with the scorching heat. With only David Beckham and Owen Hargreaves plying their trade outside the Premiership, the squad was not accustomed to the climate they faced in Portugal. Neville was particularly pleased with his contribution for England's third goal against the Swiss, but felt he had more to give offensively in future games. Some of his bursting runs had been impossible due to the heat, but he was pleased with the way the team was playing. He and his team-mates could look ahead to the final group game against Croatia full of confidence.

Thus far the tournament had failed to throw forward a clear favourite, but Neville knew that most teams would take time to hit top form. As he explained to the media: 'It's not the time to be grabbing it [the tournament] by the scruff of the neck, it's still early days.' He also revealed that the squad had been watching plenty of the other games as a way of scouting future opponents, observing their strengths and weaknesses. Neville knew the significance of this, explaining: 'Every team is a potential opponent, it's important that you watch.'

When asked about which nations had looked most impressive thus far, Neville said: 'Teams have shown glimpses. I think the heat's a big problem.'

England's final group fixture was against Croatia. Neville's appearance for England in this match put him in the history books for the most games for his country in European Championships – ten. A further boost for Gary came from Steve McClaren, the England assistant manager, who told the media that having Neville available would make a big difference to the team's chances of success. He said: 'We missed him in Japan. He is not only a great player on the field; he also provides great leadership out there. He is a great communicator and off the field he is very influential around the team. His experience of playing at the top level is invaluable.' McClaren also confirmed the crucial role Neville had played in rallying the players after the cruel loss to France in their opening group game when morale was low in the England camp. Having been through so much in his career, Gary was able to rouse his team-mates by putting the situation into perspective – they were not out of the tournament and had played very well. He let the players know there was plenty left for them to play for.

In a match in which England needed just a point to qualify, Croatia were soundly beaten 4–2. Wayne Rooney was shining as a star for the future and his goals were proving the catalyst for good team performances. Paul Scholes, who had suffered a three-year goal drought for England, was back on the scoresheet against Croatia and optimism swept the country once again. Having secured the runners-up position in the group, England progressed to face Portugal, the competition's host nation. Neville would be facing Cristiano Ronaldo, his United team-mate. Gary spoke to the media prior to the game and spoke of his excitement about the quarter-final: 'I'm looking forward to the game, but I'm not sure I'm looking forward to facing Cristiano Ronaldo! I've faced him every day in training this season and he can embarrass you. I know on Thursday that I'm not going to get one single second's rest while he's on the field.'

Neville believed that England could compete with Portugal and knew that, while the Portuguese side was brimming with quality, England had enough match-winners to go into the quarter-final full of confidence. It was the sort of confident statement the nation was crying out for – a player who was prepared to give honest answers. Clearly, the players were aware of the great hope among England supporters back home, because Neville commented to the media: 'It's impossible to keep our nation level-headed. We lose a game, they all want us hung up; we win a game, they all want us knighted. That's the way it is in England.' But the players tried to put the excitement of the nation to one side as they focused on the match.

However, it was the same old story for England's brave players. Neville and his team-mates put in a gutsy display, but were eliminated from yet another tournament on penalties. The big turning point came when Wayne Rooney had to leave the field through injury. England had taken the lead through Michael Owen who, along with Rooney, had troubled the Portuguese defenders early on, but when Rooney limped off just before the half-hour mark, the momentum swung in Portugal's favour. England still kept the host nation at bay until the eighty-third minute when Helder Postiga, who had been a flop at Tottenham, headed home with the England back four defending a cross far too deep in the area.

England fought back and Neville thought they had won it when Sol Campbell put the ball in the net, but referee Urs Meier blew for a dubious foul by John Terry on the Portuguese goalkeeper. Extra-time was another shining example of England's character as, despite going behind to a Rui Costa strike, Neville and his team-mates fought back to equalise through Frank Lampard. And so it came down to spot-kicks once more. David Beckham got England off to the worst possible start as he blazed over but, in his defence, the penalty spot was far from adequate for a crucial international shootout. Rui Costa's missed penalty brought the scores level and, after five kicks, it was 4–4. Darius Vassell stepped up for England's first sudden-death kick but saw his penalty saved by Ricardo, who unbelievably sent the next Portugal player away so that he could have the chance to score the winning spot-kick himself. Ricardo slotted home his penalty and Portugal were through to the semi-finals, the first time they had ever reached that stage of a major international tournament.

The heartbreak was written all over Gary's face after the defeat. It was his second experience of penalty elimination and it is undoubtedly the harshest way to lose a football match. England had performed well to keep Portugal at bay and Neville refused to look for excuses. It was simply bad luck in the shootout once more. He did, though, point to two crucial moments that went against England – the injury to Wayne Rooney and the disallowed goal from Sol Campbell. He knew Portugal had not deserved to lose either and so a penalty shootout was the only way to settle the contest, but for England it was the cruellest way to go out of the tournament. Surely FIFA must search for a fairer alternative to the shootout for deciding drawn matches because, ultimately, penalties are simply a lottery.

A further sad note was that this turned out to be Paul Scholes' last appearance in an England shirt and his retirement from international football in August 2004 was a major blow. Scholes explained to the press: 'I have been considering retiring from international football for a while. Euro 2004 was fantastic, but afterwards I felt the time was right for myself and my family to make it my last England appearance.' Neville's United team-mate had been asked to play out of position on the left-hand side at times and there were suggestions that Scholes simply did not enjoy international football as much as he enjoyed playing for United. Either way, Gary was sorry to see one of the finest midfielders of his generation retiring from the international scene at only twenty-nine years of age.

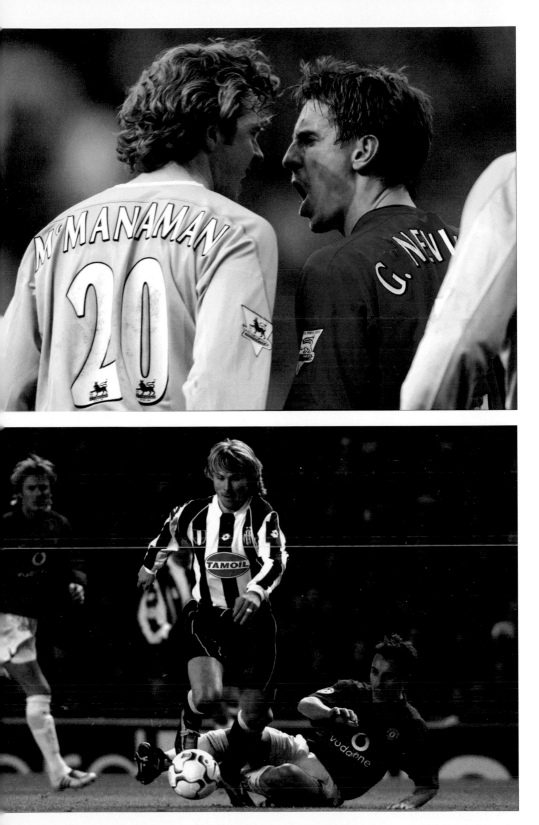

Gary's renowned as a competitive player who's never been afraid to get stuck in and battle for his team.

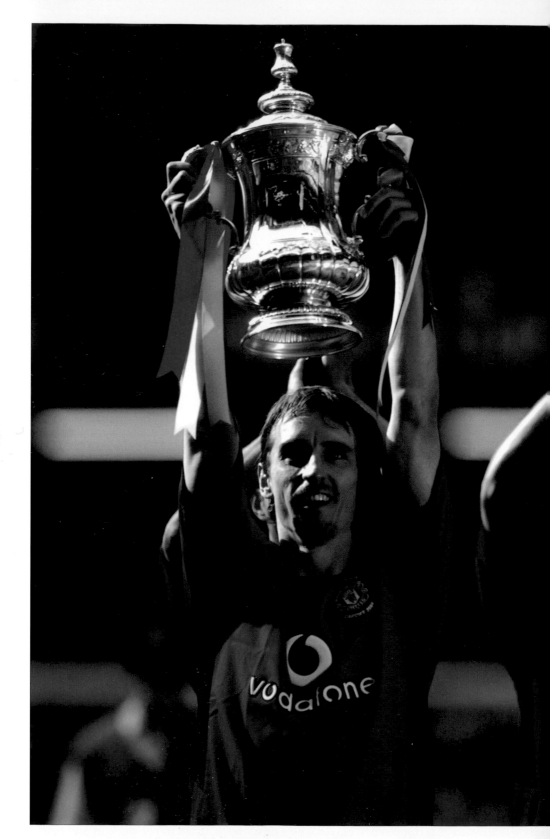

Neville lifts the FA Cup in 2004 – the third time he'd won it at Man Utd.

Gary has a special respect for his boss Sir Alex Ferguson, built up over many years. Club captain after Roy Keane's departure in December 2005, Gary is one of his gaffer's staunchest lieutenants.

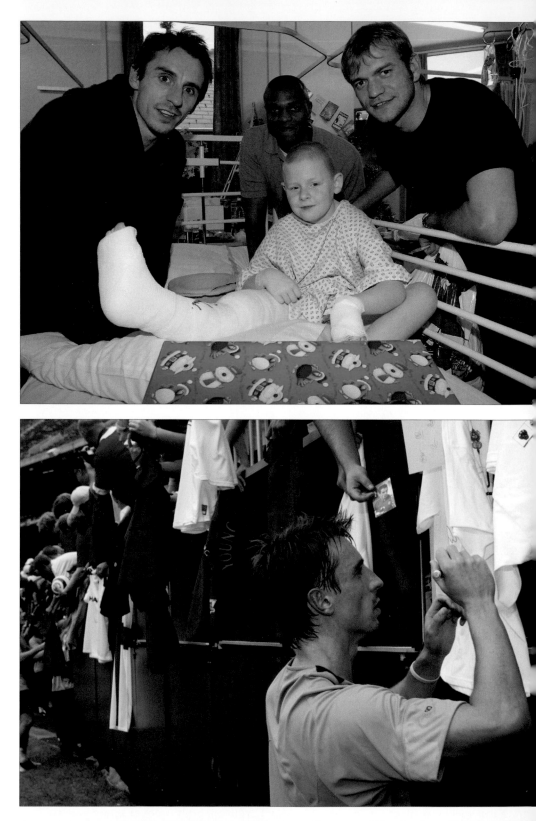

A great ambassador for his club, Gary's happy to give something back to the Man Utd fans away from the pitch.

Doing some not-so-serious relaxing with Man Utd team-mates and turning on the glamour at a charity do, ably assisted by his fiancée Emma Hadfield.

Now a senior player in the England set-up, Gary's a key figure upon whom a lot of responsibility is placed both on and off the pitch, as shown during World Cup 2006.

Gary surges forward from the back in the hothouse arena of the quarter-final in
Gelsenkirchen against Portugal at the 2006 World Cup.

Looking ahead, Gary has vowed to make himself available to club and country as long as his services continue to be called upon – and there's no sign of his defensive strengths waning for years to come.

Chapter 8

The Arrival of the Special One

The summer of 2004 signalled the beginning of a new era in Premiership football. Though no one knew it for sure at the time, Jose Mourinho's arrival in England as Chelsea manager would add a new element to the title race. Having led unfancied FC Porto to Champions League glory the previous season, Mourinho was headhunted by Chelsea to take over from Claudio Ranieri and push the team forward as genuine title challengers. Abramovich's first season in England had seen Chelsea impress, reaching the semi-finals of the European Cup, a run that included eliminating rivals Arsenal. Chelsea also finished second in the Premiership, albeit eleven points behind the title-winning Gunners. For most this represented significant improvement, but it was not enough for Abramovich, so he and Ranieri parted company and Jose Mourinho was recruited to take charge.

Mourinho had begun his career in football as both assistant coach and interpreter to Bobby Robson, working with the Englishman at Sporting Lisbon and FC Porto. The duo then moved to Barcelona in 1996 where the team won the UEFA Cup-Winners' Cup in 1996–97. Mourinho later decided to try his hand at management himself and, after a spell coaching Barcelona B, he took charge of Benfica. He lasted only nine games before quitting but, in January 2002, another opportunity fell into Mourinho's lap and he was appointed as manager of FC Porto. His success there is well-documented as he won back-to-back league titles, the UEFA Cup in 2003 as well as the Champions League in 2004. When Chelsea announced that Jose Mourinho was their new manager, Neville knew the Blues meant business.

The new Chelsea manager stunned Neville and football fans all over the country with his confidence as he was unveiled at Stamford Bridge. Speaking to the media, he was very assured: 'We have top players and, sorry if I'm arrogant, but we now have a top manager. The English Premiership is recognised as the best league in the world and I am really excited at the prospect of competing week in, week out at the highest level in England as well as in Europe.' Mourinho also admitted: 'I think I am a special manager because I have won the Champions League.' Thus, the nickname the 'Special One' was born.

While Ranieri had received criticism for some of his tactics and squad rotation, it seemed that Abramovich had now got a man who would get everything spot on, and the Chelsea players quickly expressed their liking for the new regime. Inevitably, more big-money faces arrived at Stamford Bridge in the summer of 2004 as Mourinho looked to put his own stamp on the team. Goalkeeper Petr Cech was signed to challenge Carlo Cudicini for the No. 1 jersey; defenders Paulo Ferreira and Ricardo Carvalho made the journey from Porto with Mourinho; and left-winger Arjen Robben was added to the attack after snubbing Manchester United. Mourinho also strengthened the front line with Mateja Kezman from PSV Eindhoven and Didier Drogba from Olympique Marseille. It was a warning sign to their title rivals, whose transfer-market activity was significant but certainly not as extravagant.

United strengthened their squad over the summer with three big signings that Sir Alex Ferguson hoped would address their woes from the previous season. Alan Smith, the physical, passionate forward, was bought from relegated Leeds United; defender Gabriel Heinze, relatively unknown to most, was signed from Paris St Germain, and then there was Wayne Rooney. In a bold move, Ferguson splashed out £27 million on the teenager in a bid to compete with the ever-improving Chelsea squad. It was a hugely prolonged chase, but United eventually got the player they felt could be a star at the highest level for over a decade.

Neville, who had played alongside Rooney in the summer at Euro 2004 in Portugal, was delighted with the news. He noted the signing had lifted the mood around the club and that excitement surrounded the squad. In Rooney, United had bought a player capable of lighting up any game. Gary also recognised that, like so many young stars, there was already a lot of media pressure on the young player. In an England press conference he said: 'He's a fantastic player, but I don't want to say too much about him because there's so much out there and it amazes me the attention he gets. It was the same a bit when David Beckham was at United, and you don't need your fellow players adding to it. But we all know how good he is.' It was also a big summer for Neville himself because he signed a new five-year contract with United – a deal that meant he would probably see out the rest of his career at the club. There was no doubt in Gary's mind when it came to signing on the dotted line: he could never leave the club he loved so much. United supporters will hope he can maintain his fitness levels and play on beyond his current contract, which ends in 2009.

It is common for United to begin a campaign in sloppy fashion, but 2004–05 started so miserably that Chelsea and Arsenal were able to build a strong advantage over Neville and his colleagues early in the season. The problems were already apparent in the FA Community Shield, as Arsenal's youngsters humbled United 3–1, highlighting the lack of quality young players bursting onto the scene at Old Trafford compared with the immense potential of Gunners stars like Cesc Fabregas. Neville and his youth-team colleagues had certainly set the bar very high, but it was still surprising that the youth system had not provided more talent in the past few seasons.

As luck would have it, the opening-day fixtures saw Manchester United travel to London to face Jose Mourinho's Chelsea. Ferguson and Mourinho had been involved in a row during the United-FC Porto Champions League tie the previous season, so it was a game both managers were desperate to win. Neville found himself playing in a side depleted through injury, and with Roy Keane and Quinton Fortune lining up alongside him in a makeshift defence for the Chelsea game, it was far from an ideal start. Chelsea took their chance to add to United's misery, beating them 1–0 through an Eidur Gudjohnsen goal to make it a memorable first taste of the Premiership for Mourinho. Three consecutive draws against Blackburn, Everton and Bolton had the critics busy once more as United's season struggled to get off the ground but, with a mountain of injuries in the squad, Neville and his team-mates had to battle on.

*****

The international break came as a welcome release for Neville. The team gathered to take on Austria and Poland in the first two fixtures of their World Cup qualifying group. A 3–0 friendly win over Ukraine had been good preparation for the opening qualifier away to Austria and Neville, after the disappointment of the past two international tournaments, had re-focused his mind and had moved on from the disappointment of Euro 2004.

Neville was always very supportive of Sven-Goran Eriksson, despite the public's growing frustration with the Swede and, prior to the Austria game, he publicly defended Eriksson in front of the media, saying: 'I think we have got as good a manager as England could possibly have. I genuinely believe that. He's created a calm around the team and the players believe in him. I think the fans believe in him, too – the reception that both the players and he get everywhere shows that.'

Gary insisted that Eriksson's record deserved more credit, considering that England had only lost two competitive matches in normal time during his spell in charge – against France and Brazil. He felt the team had progressed massively under Eriksson and could not believe the calls for the manager to be sacked. Neville was insistent that keeping faith with Eriksson was vital for the team: 'We should have a football manager for England for a long period of time who can bring continuity and stability. That's the way success is always bred. We're not going to have a chance if we keep changing our manager every year and a half.'

The sadness of the Euro 2004 exit was clearly difficult to remove from the players' minds, but Neville urged the squad to focus on the job in hand. He admitted that every day during the tournament he had felt that England would win it, but the squad would have to wait two years for their next chance. In the meantime, he wanted everyone to concentrate on the qualifying campaign.

Eriksson, so often criticised towards the end of his spell as England manager, brought his own style of management to the job and Neville had nothing but praise for his approach. The manager was rarely seen showing emotion on the touchline, but Gary felt this was Eriksson's strength, because the Swede had managed to keep everyone in the England set-up calm ahead of big games. He was disappointed that everyone interpreted Eriksson's calm demeanour as a sign that he did not care about the job.

As he gave this glowing report on Eriksson, Neville was certainly suggesting that some of the previous England managers had flaws in their managerial techniques – whether it was tactical faults or problems with man-management. Gary claimed that Eriksson had 'removed the nonsense and the silliness that has affected some England managers over the last ten, twenty, thirty years'. But other senior England players came out with more critical assessments of Eriksson's spell as manager of the national team.

The Austria match was another sad story for Neville and England. A 2–2 draw represented two points dropped and the result put more pressure on Eriksson and the underperforming players. Leading 2–0 through goals from Lampard and Gerrard, England squandered their advantage, with David James at fault for Austria's second goal. The media was quick to pour scorn on the performance, and on James in particular. This prompted the second media boycott of Neville's international career (after the 1-0 loss to Germany at Wembley being the first) as the players rallied behind James against some of the harsh criticisms. A win over Poland went some way to silencing the doubters and four points from two away games represented a decent start to England's World Cup campaign.

Neville rejoined his United team-mates knowing that significant improvements were required. United's early-season problems were largely caused by their long injury list. The team was missing a number of key players. Deprived of Rio Ferdinand, Wes Brown, Gabriel Heinze, Roy Keane, Ole Gunnar Solskjaer, Ruud van Nistelrooy and Wayne Rooney from some of their early fixtures, United had been left vulnerable and opposition sides had seized their chance to punish them. Neville, too, had an enforced period on the sidelines due to a hairline fracture of his kneecap sustained on international duty against Poland. Inconsistency continued to hinder the team's title prospects as Arsenal lengthened their unbeaten run.

A victory against Liverpool at Old Trafford marked the return to action of Rio Ferdinand following his eight-month drugs ban and, ten days later, Wayne Rooney was back to full fitness – and back with a bang. Rooney finally made his Manchester United debut against

Fenerbache in the Champions League group stage and made the best possible start to his career as a Red by netting a brilliant hat-trick. The game also marked Neville's return to action, but that went rather unnoticed as Rooney deservedly grabbed the headlines. Gary was taken aback by the youngster's stunning start, especially considering Rooney was coming back from injury. The former Everton man had made an immediate impact and had showed no signs of rustiness after his layoff.

Neville was also very quick to praise Ferdinand's comeback and the way he had handled the difficult patch: 'I really didn't think anybody could show the professionalism he has shown over that eight months. If you take a Saturday game away from a football player then, in my mind, you are taking away their life – and that's what happened to him for eight months. So the professionalism he showed was fantastic.' Ferdinand's commitment to the club earned him a lot of respect from the management and his fellow players. What's more, everyone was delighted to have such a talented defender available for selection again.

Gary lined up for England in two qualifiers in October. The team continued to progress steadily without producing the quality performances they were clearly capable of. Narrow wins over Wales and Azerbaijan may have yielded six points, but the anti-Eriksson feeling was building with every sloppy display. The Swede's popularity had reached an incredible peak after the 5–1 win in Germany and the automatic qualification from the group, but his inability to take England beyond the quarter-finals of a major tournament, despite the abundant talent of the squad, saw the public start to turn against him.

In the Premiership, draws with Middlesbrough and Birmingham were hardly the desired preparation for the visit of Arsenal to Old Trafford on 24 October. The Gunners had continued their unbeaten run from the previous season and, while the build-up was far from ideal, the chance to end Arsenal's unbeaten record was motivation enough for the players. Gary and his brother Phil led the aggressive approach United brought into the game, seemingly picking out Jose Antonio Reyes for particular attention. The Spaniard had been impressive in the Community Shield and Gary looked to stick tighter to him and limit his touches. The game was as tight as everyone expected, but it was United who emerged with the three points through a Ruud van Nistelrooy penalty (controversially awarded for a Sol Campbell challenge) and a Wayne Rooney strike. It was a massive win for United and it threw Arsenal off course to such an extent that it ultimately ruined their season. Arsenal's form dipped dramatically following the Old Trafford defeat and Chelsea were able to overtake them at the top of the table.

The match will, of course, be remembered for ending Arsenal's unbeaten record on forty-nine games – perhaps it was only right that it was United, their biggest rivals, who finally won against the Gunners. But the after-match antics will always be recalled along with the result. The media tagged the match 'Battle of the Buffet', as a melee in the tunnel saw the United manager Sir Alex Ferguson struck in the face with a slice of pizza thrown by an Arsenal player amid rowing and scuffling involving both sets of players and the two managers. The rivalry between the two clubs had reached a new high. The commotion and bans of the previous season had been trumped by this new chapter in the feud. The win put United eight points behind Arsenal and reignited the players' hopes of clawing their way back into the title race. But, in an example of their struggles, United travelled to Fratton Park in the next league game and were beaten 2–0 by Portsmouth.

Amid an already packed fixture list, Neville and England took on Spain on 17 November in a chaotic friendly, losing 1–0. The defeat away to Spain did little to help the England team as Wayne Rooney had to be subbed off to avoid an imminent red card and Ashley Cole and Shaun Wright-Phillips were subjected to racist chants. Another friendly was organised for 9 February against Holland. It was a fairly uneventful 0–0 draw, but the fixture promoted the anti-racism campaign, with both teams wearing kits displaying the message. While in full support of the sentiment, aspects of the initiative upset Neville, who feared that sports companies were using the campaign to gain free publicity. He explained his concerns to the media: 'We have to make sure it's conducted in the right manner and not done just for PR.

The FA and the England team have always campaigned against racism very well, we have just got to be aware that it is not cheapened slightly by companies getting a lot of PR out of it for nothing.' Further victories in late March over weaker opponents Northern Ireland and Azerbaijan in the qualifying group kept England on course for top spot, but the performances were still lacking the fluidity England supporters expected.

*****

For United, November and December proved more fruitful months as they finally began to string quality displays together. Four consecutive victories in the league against Newcastle, Charlton, West Brom and Southampton eased the team back into form, but Gary was unfortunate to suffer an illness that ruled him out of the last two matches in December and he was unable to return to the starting line-up until 19 January. As usual, United's form had picked up as the New Year approached, but Chelsea and Arsenal still held the advantage. As United continued to trail the top two, Neville could not help but respect the form Chelsea had shown and the impressive ruthless streak they had developed, particularly in away games. He noted that the Blues had been finishing teams off – something United had struggled to do – and he urged United to put a good run of form together. It was a tough time for everyone at the club. Neville had been fortunate enough to experience so much success with the Reds, but now he was enduring a barren spell. The consistency in United's performances was missing and, while they remained in the top three, Neville and his team-mates quickly fell too far behind leaders Chelsea.

The Champions League had proved more successful for United than the Premiership. Placed in a group with Lyon, Fenerbahce and Sparta Prague, United lost just one of the six group matches to finish in second place behind Lyon. Gary added to his goal tally with the opening goal against the French side at Old Trafford in their 2–1 win, firing home from close range when their opponents failed to clear. The performances had not been fantastic, but the players had done enough to earn a spot in the draw for the knockout rounds. With United's league form faltering, the Champions League took on an even greater significance for Neville and his team-mates.

Following on from their success in Europe, the team's domestic displays improved dramatically. United produced an excellent series of results over the Christmas period – so often crucial to the title race – and the mood at Old Trafford became less gloomy. Wins over Crystal Palace, Bolton, Aston Villa and Middlesbrough meant United had taken maximum points during the congested Christmas fixture list. If only they had begun the season so well. Neville hoped it would be a launching pad for the rest of the campaign.

January was another good month for United as the

team won at Anfield and booked their place in the FA Cup fifth round. The only negative was their Carling Cup semi-final defeat to Chelsea, which was a blow for Neville, who had another trip to the Millennium Stadium in his sights. Having drawn the first leg at Stamford Bridge, it was disappointing to lose the return leg at home. Undoubtedly, Jose Mourinho's Chelsea side were enjoying the edge over United this season.

The second Premiership meeting between Manchester United and Arsenal yet again lived up to all the hype in a compelling fixture at Highbury. Pre-match, Neville stated that if United won then it would give them extra confidence to really make Chelsea nervy at the top, but he knew it would take a good performance to pick up the three points away to the Gunners. It was destined to be a tense affair. The feuding was evident even prior to kick-off as confrontations in the tunnel boiled over as Patrick Vieira and Roy Keane had a verbal spat. Sky Sports pictures captured some of the unrest and it turned out that Neville was at the centre of the dispute. It is believed that Vieira was baiting Neville – reports suggest he aggressively claimed that Neville would not kick Arsenal all over the pitch again (referring to Gary's physical marking of Jose Antonio Reyes in the clubs' previous encounter) – and at this point Keane stepped in to support his team-mate. The essence of Keane's argument was that if Vieira wanted to pick on a United player, then he should try Keane. Just minutes before such a massive clash, the message of togetherness sent out by Keane proved perfect motivation for United to deliver a solid performance and, at times, tear Arsenal to shreds.

However, it was only in the second half that United gained a full grip on the match. They trailed twice in the first half to goals from Vieira and Dennis Bergkamp, but their persistence brought them level at 2–2 through Cristiano Ronaldo, who also grabbed the third to put United ahead. A late John O'Shea goal sealed the victory and Gary was thrilled with the three points. The frustrating fact, though, for Neville was that if the team had played like this throughout the campaign, they would have been closer to the top of the table. Inevitably, though, the victory was overshadowed by Keane's pre-match clash with Vieira.

Roy Keane gave his typically blunt version of events. In an interview, he told the BBC: 'If people want to intimidate some of our team-mates, let's have a go at some of their players. They think Gary Neville is an easy target, but I'm not having it.' To have a captain stand up for his team so publicly in the build-up to such a huge match must have lifted the United players. But then that is Keane all over. Neville has always held Keane in the highest esteem as an inspirational skipper and a complete midfielder – the type nobody enjoys facing.

Responding to the validity of Keane's account of the pre-match argument, Neville diplomatically said, 'Roy Keane's not a liar. There were a couple of things that did happen before the game that disappoint you, especially from players of that calibre. You can talk about spirit all you want, but that was spirit we showed out on the pitch.' The bottom line was that, on a night of highly charged emotion, United had outplayed a very talented Arsenal line-up. Henry Winter, of the *Daily Telegraph*, expressed his admiration for United's determination, saying: 'This compelling, sulphurous affair signified everything to Manchester United. Inspired by Roy Keane, and the expert finishing of Cristiano Ronaldo, they came from behind to move ahead of Arsenal into second. Losing was simply not in the lexicon of United's ten hungry men last night.'

Arsene Wenger had claimed pre-match that the loser would be out of the title race. After the defeat, a downcast Wenger was true to his word and declared his side were out of the race: 'Manchester United still have a small chance, but for us it's over.' Ferguson's reaction, in contrast to the shattered Wenger, was very upbeat. While he admitted Chelsea were still in the driving seat, he was pleased with his team's efforts. After the match he told the media: 'We can win every game and not win the title and it's as simple as that. Chelsea are in a great position. The important thing is we have shown great form and we must have a chance.'

In contrast to their previous meeting in October, when the win against Arsenal failed to bring a run of wins, this triumph saw United begin a run of eight league and cup games without defeat and four consecutive victories. Neville had explained in numerous interviews, such as in mid-December and after the 4–2 win at Highbury, that the title race was still alive and that United were producing the type of end-of-season form for which they are so famous. Gary was especially pleased with the team's win in the Manchester derby on 13 February. The FA Cup was looking promising for United as they overcame Everton 2–0 at Goodison Park in the fifth round and then hammered Southampton 4–0 at St Mary's to book their place in the semi-finals.

The second-round draw for the Champions' League paired United with Italian giants AC Milan. This would represent a real test of the team's pedigree against probably the most experienced side in the competition. The first leg at Old Trafford was a bitterly disappointing night. United played well, kept Milan at bay and threatened to score several times, but the Italians were always menacing, with Andrea Pirlo, Rui Costa and Kaka all linking up neatly in midfield. With twelve minutes remaining, AC Milan struck their sucker punch. Roy Carroll fumbled a Clarence Seedorf strike and Hernan Crespo was on hand to smash home a priceless away goal and silence a disbelieving Old Trafford crowd. It was cruel on United and it left them with a mountain to climb in the second leg.

The return leg proved another sad night for Neville. It was a revealing statistic about United's season that this was only the second time that Sir Alex Ferguson had been able to field Ruud van Nistelrooy, Ryan Giggs, Wayne Rooney, Cristiano Ronaldo and Paul Scholes in the same game – the first being the win over Arsenal in

October. Having played in the first leg, Neville missed the game in the San Siro and had to watch on as Paolo Maldini and his team-mates put in another secure defensive display. Again United created several chances, but it was Crespo who popped up with the goal once again as Milan closed out the tie with another 1–0 win. It was a frustrating exit for United and it highlighted how they were lacking wily experience in Europe, something Milan had in abundance. Ferguson summed up the two games perfectly in his post-match interview: 'The margins at this level are very fine and that is what has decided the tie overall. I'm disappointed to go out, but we've gone out to a very good team.'

Sloppiness marred United's Premiership run-in as April proved a poor month for the club. Draws against Crystal Palace and Birmingham were simply not good enough for a team chasing the title and a 2–0 defeat at Carrow Road against Norwich summed up United's shortcomings. A 1–0 loss away to Everton was certainly a low point for Neville as he picked up a red card for kicking the ball into the crowd. It was ruled to have been dangerous and seemed to be in response to abuse from the Everton supporters. Sir Alex Ferguson said that Neville should have known better and it was an incident Neville himself will want to forget. He received a three-match ban, but it could have been worse as, at one stage, extra punishment was being considered and Merseyside Police became involved in the saga.

There would be no last-day dramatics at the top of the

Premiership as the Blues sealed the title on 30 April, but United played their part in the tense relegation dogfight. Four teams – Norwich, Southampton, Crystal Palace and West Brom – reached the final day of the season with a chance of survival and three of them would go down to the Championship. It was an incredible finale. United faced Southampton at St Mary's and, despite going behind, won the game 2–1, relegating their opponents in the process. Remarkably, it was West Brom, who had been bottom of the table at Christmas and eight points from safety, who escaped relegation; it was the first time a club had survived after being bottom at Christmas.

United progressed to face Arsenal in the FA Cup final with a 4–1 semi-final win over Newcastle at the Millennium Stadium. Neville thoroughly enjoyed the win and it kept United on course for silverware. Ruud van Nistelrooy struck a brace, ending a fairly miserable spell in front of goal for the Dutchman. As Gary prepared himself for yet another cup final, the nation waited in anticipation for another United-Arsenal clash. In the Premiership, Mourinho and Chelsea delivered their final blow to United with a 3–1 win at Old Trafford, setting a new Premiership points tally record of ninety-four. Mourinho was gracious in victory and, like Neville and United, he looked forward to the next title race. Despite United's victory over Arsenal at Highbury, after which Wenger ruled his side out of the title race, Arsenal finished the season in second place with a strong run of results in the closing weeks. It set everything up perfectly for the teams' third and final meeting of the campaign.

All that remained for United and Arsenal was the FA Cup final, a chance for both of them to salvage something from the season. With Chelsea confirmed as Premiership champions and Liverpool in the Champions League final, the two biggest sides from the past decade were forced to battle it out for the FA Cup. But for Neville, the season was over. A groin injury meant he only made the bench for the showcase final and did not enter the fray. Missing a match of this magnitude came as a huge disappointment, but he cheered on his colleagues with all his usual gusto. It was an enthralling contest as United dominated for large parts of the contest without finding the net. Wayne Rooney and Ruud van Nistelrooy both came close to breaking the deadlock, but when 120 minutes of football could not separate the two sides, the game went to penalties. Jens Lehmann emerged as the hero as he saved a Paul Scholes penalty and Patrick Vieira slotted home the winning spot-kick. It was a bitter blow for United who had battered Arsenal on the day in a clear signal of intent for next season. Cristiano Ronaldo and Rooney gave Arsenal full-backs Lauren and Ashley Cole a torrid afternoon, while Roy Keane proved more impressive than Vieira in their central-midfield tussle. It was undoubtedly a game United should have won, but luck deserted them and too many good chances were spurned. Nevertheless, United had shown that the hunger, which had led them to so many successes both domestically and in Europe, was still there and that they would be a force to be reckoned with again the following season.

Having spent around £40 million in the summer, Ferguson would have been very disappointed not to secure a trophy in the 2004–05 season. The signing of Wayne Rooney had undoubtedly been a good buy, but his decision to invest in young, unproven players had backfired, as they had struggled to make an impact in the fast-paced Premiership. Kleberson and Djemba-Djemba had contributed little since their arrival in the summer of 2003, while Liam Miller, signed to eventually replace Roy Keane, showed no signs of being selected as a first-team regular. Perhaps the biggest plus of the season, beside the contribution of Rooney, was the form of full-back Gabriel Heinze. The Argentine international had become a firm favourite at Old Trafford through his competitive, whole-hearted performances at left-back and looked a very good signing for the club. But nothing could mask the fact that United had finished third in the Premiership for the second consecutive season, and the fact that no United player had registered more than eleven league goals told the whole sorry story.

The summer saw a tour of the United States for an England squad comprised mainly of up-and-coming players. Gary was allowed to have a well-earned rest and the majority of the England first team missed the trip. Eriksson would have been pleased with the results from the two matches against the USA and then Colombia as England won both and several players pushed themselves into the reckoning for the next qualifier. For once, Neville was able to enjoy a full summer of relaxation. It was a very welcome rest. It was for these peaceful few months that Paul Scholes had decided to end his England career, thinking that the extra time to recuperate would prolong his club career at United. Gary could not dispute that a summer away from football had allowed him to return to pre-season training fresher and more driven than ever. He was desperate to ensure that United did not go a third season without winning the Premiership title.

Chapter 9

Neville, United Captain

Once again the close-season was dominated by Chelsea flexing their financial muscles in the transfer market. Having fallen short in the Champions League the previous season, Mourinho and Abramovich were out to make amends. In addition to the impressive squad Chelsea had already built, Mourinho added midfielder Michael Essien from Lyon for £24.4 million, Asier Del Horno from Athletic Bilbao for £8 million, Shaun Wright-Phillips from Manchester City for £21 million and the relatively unknown Lassana Diarra from Le Havre as a long-term replacement for Claude Makelele. In comparison, United were very restrained. Ferguson only brought in Edwin van der Sar from Fulham for a reported fee of £2 million and Ji-Sung Park from PSV Eindhoven in a £4 million deal. It was not the busy summer in the transfer market the United supporters had hoped for.

The biggest news of the summer came in the form of Malcolm Glazer's successful takeover bid that saw him become the new owner of Manchester United. The American businessman had made his name in the NFL as the owner of the Tampa Bay Buccaneers and the Glazer family had then turned their attention to United – a club that had potential to be exploited as a brand both in America and in Asia. The bid was viewed with great disapproval by many United fans and it led to mass protests. Already disillusioned by two years without a Premiership title, the news of Glazer arriving – seemingly with no interest in 'soccer' – provoked angry responses from many fans. It was thought that the high value of Manchester United would prevent any bidder from buying the club, but Glazer was able to do just that and more, as he turned United into a private company. Nobody could tell exactly what the Glazers' plans for United would be, but the vibe around the club was far from positive. It was a testing time for the United players too and was hardly ideal preparation for the new season.

The signing of van der Sar was particularly interesting, as the goalkeeper was coming to the end of his career. Yet Ferguson claimed he was the man to fill the void left by Peter Schmeichel. The United manager had tried unsuccessfully to sign van der Sar in the past and, having followed his career with interest, he now had his man. For Neville, having a goalkeeper with the domestic and

European experience of van der Sar behind him was reassuring. Schmeichel had been a massive influence on Gary's early years in the first team and United certainly missed the qualities the Dane had brought to the side – qualities that were sadly missing in the likes of Mark Bosnich, Massimo Taibi and Tim Howard.

For Gary, the summer brought the sad news that his brother Phil was going to end his time at United and move to Everton in search of more first-team opportunities. The consistent performances of Gary, Gabriel Heinze and Mikael Silvestre in the full-back positions and the quality of the United midfield meant that Phil could not hold down a regular place in the starting line-up. It was a situation that pained manager Sir Alex Ferguson, who had nurtured Phil and brought him through into the first team. But Ferguson understood Phil's reasons for needing a move. In early August, Phil explained to the media: 'This has been the most difficult decision I have ever made. I would like to thank Sir Alex, all the players and the fans for their great support.' Ferguson, cutting a dejected figure, said: 'This was not a decision we wanted to make. You couldn't meet a better professional and he leaves with the gratitude of everyone at the club for his service to United. I wish all the best to Phil and his family.'

The move was even harder for Gary to come to terms with. He had grown accustomed to having Phil alongside him whenever he was training or playing in matches. As a United supporter, it was a tough decision for Phil to turn his back on the club, but he felt it was the right move for him, especially as he needed to be playing regularly domestically in order to secure a place in the England squad. Looking back at the summer of 2005, Gary wrote in the *Times*: 'Everton got themselves one of the deals of the season when they signed Phil last summer. He has not only been a great addition to the team but, as they will have discovered, there is not a more dedicated, committed professional out there.'

After two seasons without winning the Premiership, Gary urged United to raise their game and claimed the team were ready to challenge. On the eve of the season, Neville wrote in his *Times* newspaper column on 13 August: 'The wolves are at the door of Old Trafford to judge from a lot of what has been said and written about Manchester United in pre-season. There are a lot of questions being asked of us after the change of ownership, talk of Rio Ferdinand's contract and not winning the title for two seasons.' He knew the team had to focus on the Premiership, which was looking harder than ever to win.

Neville also credited Arsenal and Chelsea for their 'fantastic seasons' in 2003–04 and 2004–05 respectively and emphasised how fine the margin for error had become. Serious title challengers could not afford to slip more than four or five points behind the leaders and so every point dropped was costly. The expectations at Old Trafford are always extremely high, but Neville felt the squad was capable of living up to the hype. With players of the calibre of van Nistelrooy, Rooney, Ronaldo and Scholes to name but a few, United were justified in feeling they could win the title.

Pre-season saw the unusual sight of United as neither favourites nor joint favourites for the title with the bookmakers – a fact remarked upon by Neville, who simply called it 'a spur'. Chelsea approached the new campaign with very open confidence, something that did not impress Gary; nor did a comment from Peter Kenyon, Chelsea's chief executive, that the Premiership would be won 'from a small group of one'. He still remembered Kenyon from his early days at United, when he would sweat abundantly in meetings with Gary, Roy Keane and Ryan Giggs. Neville hoped Kenyon would regret making such hasty predictions.

Early September brought two more international qualifying games against Wales and Northern Ireland. The players needed to put in a good performance to make amends for their 4–1 defeat in Copenhagen against Denmark in a friendly just over two weeks earlier. That result had been a nightmare start for England as Denmark, who would not even go on to qualify for the 2006 World Cup, completely outplayed them. Everyone was expecting a ruthless response and many questions were being asked about the England manager and the players. So a win was very welcome against Wales at the Millennium Stadium, although the 1–0 victory could not mask another sub-par performance and the country's worst fears were confirmed the following Wednesday when England lost 1–0 away to Northern Ireland, who put in a very determined performance to overcome a disjointed, disinterested England team. Neville was not playing in either of the two qualifiers and the team missed his steadying influence and his partnership with Beckham, who looked uncomfortable in a more central role.

The season had started in promising fashion for United with three straight victories. As luck would have it, the team began their campaign away to Everton and so Gary did not have to wait long to see how strange it would be to see Phil in the blue of Everton rather than the red of Manchester United. It was Gary who earned the family bragging rights here, though, as United collected a deserved 2–0 win. The team also overcame Aston Villa and Newcastle to maintain their solid early-season form. But the old inconsistencies of the previous two campaigns surfaced again in September as United picked up draws with Manchester City and Liverpool in the Premiership – games that in the past United have seemed more fired up for – and Blackburn left Old Trafford with a shock 2–1 victory. In the 0–0 draw at Anfield, United were unfortunate to lose skipper Roy Keane with a broken foot. Few would have believed it then, but this would be the Irishman's last competitive game in a United shirt. The team ploughed on, but their form convinced no one. Their performances against Fulham, Sunderland and Tottenham were good enough to earn seven points and they safely progressed to the fourth round of the Carling Cup. A good patch for the team was typically followed by a run of disappointing results and this was the story of their season once again.

Meanwhile, Neville and England had secured top spot in their qualifying group. After the loss to Northern Ireland, many had feared for the team's chances of winning the group, but Gary knew that wins over Austria and Poland, both home games, would put England safely through. England did enough in the two games to take the six points and gain automatic qualification. Again, Neville was absent through injury, but he watched on happily as his team-mates secured first place. The main objective, World Cup qualification, had been achieved and Eriksson preached that this was all that really mattered, but there was no hiding the fact that England had fallen short of the performances they were capable of and that the players would need to step up their displays if they were to enjoy success in Germany.

The happy mood was dampened by more problems at United. Defeats against Middlesbrough – 4–1 – in the league and Lille in the Champions League sparked more negative reviews and it seemed everyone was willing to write off the team's chances. But United bounced back in early November by defeating runaway leaders Chelsea 1–0 at Old Trafford in a match that showed they could still, on their day, compete with the Blues.

Neville, forced to watch from the sidelines due to injury, was triumphant after the win, claiming the team had shown their potential. He wrote a very upbeat article in the *Times* in early November 2005 saying: 'It's been a very difficult week at Manchester United, but this result shows we can come through anything. The fans at the end were singing a song called "We'll Never Die" and I genuinely believe that is the spirit of Manchester United. It never dies, this club.' The result certainly seemed to bring confidence back to the side and Neville was full of praise for the performance. The players had shown that, at their best, they could compete with Chelsea. Gary also claimed that United had not given up hope of clawing back the title, provided they learned from Chelsea's ability to overcome weaker opponents consistently. It was only November and there was still a long way to go.

Neville pointed to the Charlton game two weekends later as an important match to show their improved consistency, but a much more significant incident caused chaos at the club on the Friday before the game at The Valley. United captain Roy Keane sensationally and controversially quit the club, as problems that had been brewing for weeks finally boiled over. While Keane's exit was announced as a decision reached by 'mutual consent', it is believed that several issues went on behind the scenes. Firstly, Keane launched into a scathing attack on four of his team-mates in the wake of the 4–1 loss to Middlesbrough on 29 October. Keane's analysis, due to be shown on MUTV – the club's own television station – was withdrawn from the schedule, replaced coincidentally by *Gary Neville Plays The Pundit*. In addition, Keane and Sir Alex Ferguson's number two, Carlos Quieroz, had been involved in a long-running row; a row that Harry Harris at the *Daily Express* said 'only increased the tension built up by the censored MUTV video'.

Harris also explained that the whole situation 'led to Sir Alex [Ferguson] and Keane having such a furious clash that the manager felt he had to act' and that Keane attacked Quieroz's coaching abilities. Interestingly, Harris even suggested at this stage that Neville was the favourite to take over as club captain. The Keane saga dominated the headlines, taking the gloss off what had been a solid series of results for the club. In his absence, and with Paul Scholes out of action with an eye problem, United turned to youngsters John O'Shea and Darren Fletcher to fill the gaping hole in midfield. Keane had actually been out of action for several weeks already and the young midfielders had begun to find their feet, with Fletcher scoring the winner against Chelsea.

There is no doubt that the departure of Keane hit the United players hard. In Neville's opinion, Keane had been the best midfielder of his generation and the Irishman's influence at Old Trafford had helped the whole squad to improve. Gary devoted part of his newspaper column in November 2005 to Keane's phenomenal attributes: 'Even when you thought you were giving 100 per cent, he would somehow squeeze another ten [percent] out of you. People compare him to Patrick Vieira, but they were worlds apart in terms of the influence they exerted on their teams.' Neville recalled one particular story that highlights Keane's character. Gary sent out a text message saying, 'This is Gary Neville's new mobile number.' Moments later, he received a reply from Keane saying, 'So what?' This was the dry sense of humour Keane brought to the dressing-room. Few better players have ever graced Old Trafford.

*****

As always, Neville was looking to the future and was encouraged by the fact that the team had recovered in the past from the departure of top players like Eric Cantona and Peter Schmeichel. Though it was a sad time for everyone connected with United, the club and Roy Keane both needed to move on.

Without David Beckham, Nicky Butt and Phil Neville, there was a distinct lack of homegrown talent in the United first team. Ryan Giggs, of course, was still producing some superb performances and John O'Shea was being used by Sir Alex Ferguson in both defence and midfield, but apart from those two, Neville has been the only regular local lad in the first team over the past couple of seasons. Worryingly, very few new young faces have broken into the first-team squad in recent times at Old Trafford and Ferguson has been forced to look to the foreign market for a lot of his signings.

So when Roy Keane and Manchester United decided to go their separate ways, it was clear that the club would be appointing a new captain for the future. Ferguson revealed that he had formed a shortlist of three for the captaincy – Neville, van Nistelrooy and Giggs – and eventually chose Neville. The manager was full of praise for everything Neville had done in his career: 'He has improved more quickly than anyone else at the club in the last two or three years. He is so consistent now, and his experience helps with that. We have a very young squad, so I had to look at someone who has been through the course and who gets respect for the years he has spent here.'

Neville's excellent service to United cannot ever be doubted and his involvement with the club at all levels has been fantastic. Ferguson revealed that Gary had helped young players over the years with all sorts of issues – such as their contracts – and he was now a hugely established figure at the club. The United manager added: 'The great thing about Gary is his fantastic character. Altogether, his attitude, character and service to the team have been outstanding for the last ten years, and that made it easy for me, really. As a professional, there are very few as good as him. His career at United has been about professionalism, good behaviour patterns, and being strong-minded and committed – he gets ten out of ten on all those points.' Neville simply stood for everything the club stood for. Van Nistelrooy put any disappointment he may have felt behind him and spoke in support of the decision to award the captain's armband to Neville. He told the press: 'I think Gary is the perfect captain for our team. He has been at the club his whole life, he has won everything in football and has great experience and great character. You can't wish for any more in a captain.'

Neville's groin injury had forced him to sit out the first half of the 2005–06 season and Ferguson experimented with several captains with Giggs, van Nistelrooy, Scholes and Ferdinand all taking a turn in charge of the team. Perhaps rather than convincing Ferguson to choose one of them, it merely confirmed the idea in the United manager's mind that Neville was the man to lead the team. It was an honour Gary had always desired and it was another childhood ambition realised. But there was a huge burden of expectation for him to lead the club to the successes of the past. Following in the footsteps of Bryan Robson, Steve Bruce, Eric Cantona and Roy Keane – to name just a few – and joining such an elite list was a special reward for the devotion he had shown to the club. The overwhelming majority of United fans were happy with the appointment of Neville as captain. Being a supporter of the club all his life, he really stood for the values of the club. A few would have preferred a bigger name, perhaps van Nistelrooy or Giggs, but no one could claim that Gary was not dedicated to the United cause.

It was not an easy job to inherit. United had finished the previous season without a trophy and once again

Chelsea were taking the Premiership by storm. Ferguson's side were encountering a tough patch and the controversial Old Trafford exit of Roy Keane made matters even worse. Losing the Irishman left a big gap in the centre of midfield; it was a gap the team struggled to fill. Ferguson had not only lost Keane's captaincy but also his premier defensive midfielder and it led to another disappointing season overall, despite winning the Carling Cup with victory over Wigan – a win that completed Gary's medal collection in domestic football.

But Ferguson had no doubts about Neville. Having worked with Gary for so many years, the United manager was perfectly placed to observe Neville's leadership qualities. Neville has, for a long time, been the most prominent spokesperson among the United players and has earned the respect of all his team-mates. His determination to forge a career in football through graft rather than through pure ability stood him in good stead for the challenge of captaining the United side on a permanent basis. He had captained United before when injuries, suspensions or squad rotation had kept more senior players on the sidelines, but this was totally different. He had now been appointed the club captain of Manchester United. Clearly, Ferguson and his coaching staff had marked him out as a captain for the future from a very young age.

As Andrew Cole pointed out in his autobiography, the signs were there all along. 'Gary has always been extremely mature. His die was always cast as a leader and there is absolutely no denying that Gary must be regarded as captaincy material.' His character has taken him a long way in his career and it would be very important for him as captain. He was the complete right-back with his tackling, crossing and commitment all massive strengths and he truly deserved the honour of captaining United. Cole, like Ferguson, saw his leadership potential early and none of Neville's ex-team-mates have a negative word to say about him. He is simply a Manchester United player whose life revolves around Manchester United. His commitment to the club is immense and he knows that second best will satisfy no one at Old Trafford. In almost all the interviews he gives regarding top-of-the-table matters, he mentions that trophies are expected at Old Trafford and that the players know they must challenge for the top prizes. This understanding and attitude shows why Ferguson wanted Neville to lead the quest for silverware. The new captain and his boss were on the same wavelength from the start.

While his first season as captain did not yield a Premiership title or the Champions League crown, Neville can be pleased with the way that United overcame Liverpool to claim second place and would have been delighted with the great potential within the squad. With players of the calibre of Cristiano Ronaldo and Wayne Rooney, the team has a bright future and everyone involved with the club believes they will be able compete with Chelsea over the coming seasons. Neville will certainly not allow the standards to drop.

When he accepted the job, he knew he would have to deliver trophies. He told the media: 'The captaincy is a great honour, and the highest I could ever be given as a United player. But the only the way I will be remembered as a captain is if I am seen lifting a trophy. If not, then I will have failed and so will the team collectively.' But he claimed he would feel no additional pressure due to the huge expectations of the club. Though he was desperate to finish his career on a high, he told the media: 'The expectancy to win trophies is there all the time. It is there constantly. I am not going to worry about it. That wouldn't be helpful.' He also tried to avoid being measured against some of the phenomenal captains in United's history, suggesting that such comparisons were ridiculous. He even remarked that he did not deserve to be mentioned in the same sentence as a past captain like Eric Cantona. Instead, Neville insisted he would be himself and do the job his own way, to the best of his ability.

But while being awarded the captaincy was a great moment for Gary, these were hard times for United. The team suffered another massive disappointment when they crashed out of the Champions League in the group stage, despite being drawn in a favourable group. They ended up bottom of the table and even failed to make the UEFA Cup, a consolation prize for the third-placed team in the group. Benfica, Lille and Villarreal were all solid sides, but this was the type of group that United in their pomp would have coasted through. Instead, forced to win away to Benfica in order to qualify, the team were beaten 2–1. The humiliation was hard for Neville to accept. Prior to the Benfica game, he had publicly said that it was unthinkable for the club to be eliminated before the knockout stages; when that became a reality, it was a devastating night for Gary. He was still only regaining form and fitness after his lengthy absence and he returned to action at a difficult stage of the season for the club – amid the Keane drama and the Champions League nightmare.

After the Champions League exit and the ever-widening gap that Chelsea were enjoying in the Premiership, the cup competitions again offered a chance of redemption for United. The way in which the team responded to the European heartbreak was highly commendable. Gary and Phil went head to head again on 11 December in the second meeting of the season between United and Everton. This time the spoils were shared in a 1–1 draw. Gary left the field disappointed that United had let another two points slip away, but Phil was jubilant, having returned to Old Trafford and put in an excellent performance. But ten consecutive games unbeaten represented a solid recovery from United and this run included some impressive displays as Wigan were hammered 4–0 and Bolton beaten 4–1.

On 3 January, United travelled to Highbury, a season on from the infamous tunnel row. A tight game, with chances for both teams, ended goal-less, but it was a performance that satisfied Neville, one of the club's harshest and most honest critics. Admittedly he had wanted the three points, but there were plenty of positives to take out of the game. Indeed, United could easily have snatched the victory and Gary was happy to see the team heading in the right direction. Being a perfectionist, though, he would have been frustrated with himself for failing to hit the target with a chance late in the game. There was an odd feel to the match at Highbury as the two teams lined up against each other with nothing at stake and with no Patrick Vieira or Roy Keane in either of the starting line-ups. This inevitably took some of the spark out of the game, but Gary still dug deep to put in a gutsy performance. Commenting a few days after the game in his column, Neville explained: 'I got nutmegged once or twice in the first fifteen minutes and you can hear the shouts "Neville, you're crap!" But that is when you have to show the strength to stay in the battle. And you fight like crazy to get back on top.'

It was then the turn of the cup competitions to take centre stage. A tie away to Burton Albion of the Conference, managed by Nigel Clough, in the FA Cup third round should have presented no problems for United but, despite sending on substitutes Cristiano Ronaldo and Wayne Rooney, Burton held on for a 0–0 draw to earn a replay at the Theatre of Dreams. Neville was not playing as Ferguson looked to give some of the club's youngsters a taste of first-team action, but the United manager would have been disappointed by what he saw.

Having reached the semi-finals of the Carling Cup,

two legs against Blackburn stood between United and the final in Cardiff. Neville ignored the comments belittling the Carling Cup and was excited about the opportunity to win some silverware. He had never won the competition, despite reaching the final in 2003, and was keen to complete his medal collection. This time there was also the extra incentive of having the chance to lift his first trophy as captain. The first leg at Ewood Park was a tight affair and a 1–1 draw set up an intriguing second leg at Old Trafford. A morale-crushing 3–1 defeat away to rivals Manchester City ended a good series of results for United. Having regularly beaten City in the nineties, United were now struggling to beat their bitter nemesis. A 5–0 win in the replay against Burton Albion slightly lifted the gloom, but the result came more as a relief than a triumph. Neville wanted more; the new United captain wanted a return to the glory days.

If ever there is a game to bring out the best in Neville, it is when playing against Liverpool. The two sides met at Old Trafford on 22 January and the match took on greater significance as the two teams fought to stay in second place and remain the closest to Chelsea, in case the Blues slipped up. Although Liverpool performed impressively, United stole the three points with a 1–0 win, courtesy of a late Rio Ferdinand header. But it was Neville rather than his team-mates who stole the headlines as a result of his goal celebration. Facing the Liverpool fans, Neville clutched the United badge on his shirt and made clear his delight at United's victory. His actions were met with widespread disapproval.

Gary himself could not comprehend how his behaviour had warranted such a reaction and fought his corner in his newspaper column on 24 January, arguing: 'I struggle to believe that I have caused any grave offence with an exuberant celebration. What are you meant to do? Smile sweetly and jog back to the halfway line? Do they want a game involving robots?' Since he was four years old, Neville had dreamt of beating Liverpool with a last-gasp winner and his wish had come true. Caught up in the moment, he had produced a celebration that may have seemed somewhat out of character, but it was a reaction simply born out of a total devotion to United. Liverpool was still the biggest fixture of the season for Neville, despite the quality of Chelsea and Arsenal, and he was always fired up for clashes with the Merseyside club. When Ferdinand scored the late goal, Neville released all the pent-up tension that had built up inside him with his celebration.

Neville also highlighted the case of Robbie Fowler, who had taunted the United fans during the Manchester derby. Fowler had received no punishment from the FA and Neville believes this is the way it should be, because the banter is all part of the game, especially when it comes to local derbies. Neville received support from some quarters. Dion Fanning, writing in the *Sunday Independent*, said: 'Neville is an innocent man, entirely within his rights to celebrate and taunt football fans who are always ready to claim incitement if, after an afternoon of abusing footballers, a footballer responds in even the most gentile way.' Fanning was correct: Neville was being punished simply for having shown his emotions.

The FA, however, saw things differently, deciding that Neville deserved a £5,000 fine for his celebration. Understandably, Neville hit back. He told the media: 'I am extremely disappointed with the decision. Being a robot devoid of passion and spirit is obviously the way forward for the modern footballer.' While the fine was only a measly sum for Neville, it was the principle rather than the quantity that angered him so much. He explained: 'I know people say that £5,000 is nothing to a Premiership footballer, but I would have contested the fine if it was 50p.'

The second leg of the Carling Cup semi-final saw United progress to the final with a 2–1 victory over a resilient Blackburn side. A 3–0 win over Wolves took United into the fifth round of the FA Cup, but their league form faltered again with a sloppy 4–3 defeat against Blackburn, a side who caused United problems every time they played during the season. A 3–1 win away to Portsmouth boosted confidence before the FA Cup tie against Liverpool at Anfield for a place in the quarter-finals. Neville's presence in the United line-up brought much chanting and abusive language, especially in the aftermath of his celebration at Old Trafford after United's last-gasp winner. But Gary had no complaints, reflecting in his *Times* column a few days after the game: 'The Liverpool fans certainly let me know what they think of me on Saturday, but I had no problem with that. I expected the abuse, although I also got half a hamburger and about £4.50. It didn't stop me taking throw-ins and playing my usual game.'

The match took place on Gary's thirty-first birthday, but it was certainly not the gift or the party he would have wanted as 40,000 Liverpool fans told him exactly what they thought of him. But it was never likely that Neville would be thrown off his game by the chants of the crowd and, prior to the game, PFA chief executive Gordon Taylor admitted he knew Gary would not be fazed by the hostile atmosphere. Neville had too much experience at the highest level to let the abuse get to him and his professionalism has always been one of his strengths. Taylor suggested that, actually, there was a grudging respect for Neville among some Liverpool fans, just as United supporters reluctantly accepted the quality of Steven Gerrard and Jamie Carragher, two diehard fans of the Merseyside club.

United lost 1–0 on the day, with Peter Crouch grabbing the winner, and Neville was disappointed with their poor display. The team simply did not play well enough and Liverpool were able to pick United off far too easily. Once Liverpool went a goal ahead in front of their own supporters, it was always going to be tough for United to fight back. To make matters worse, Alan Smith picked up a horrific injury as he broke his leg and

239

dislocated his ankle as he tried to block a John Arne Riise free-kick. It was a sickening sight for Neville to witness such a popular member of the squad suffer such a nasty injury. The news that Liverpool supporters had tried to stop the ambulance leaving Anfield made Neville even more distressed. Smith's injury capped a terrible day on Merseyside for United and for Gary, who wished his team-mate well on his long road to recovery. Liverpool would go on to win the competition, beating West Ham on penalties in a thrilling FA Cup final.

There was no time for Neville and United to feel sorry for themselves, however, as Wigan awaited them in the Carling Cup final. In the past this cup competition had been snubbed by Sir Alex Ferguson, but in the past few years it had gained more interest from United as first Arsenal and then Chelsea started to dominate the Premiership. The match turned out to be one of the most one-sided, mis-matched finals in the history of English football. Wigan worked hard, but a 4–0 victory did not flatter United, who could have scored more. Neville, winning his first trophy as captain, was aware of the weight of expectation on the shoulders of the players and he told the media: 'I know how bad it feels to lose a cup final, so it was great to be reminded of how good it is to win one. People can be as cynical as they like about the Carling Cup. We put in a really good performance. We couldn't lose today. It would have been a media massacre!'

But even amid the triumphant mood at the club,

Neville remained cautious. The Carling Cup glory had been a good achievement, but Gary knew that United were expected to be competing for the Premiership and the Champions League. It was towards winning these competitions that the club needed to build and Sir Alex Ferguson seemed to have enough quality youngsters to make his vision a reality. As if still fired up from the final, United went on to win seven successive matches, starting with a 2–1 win at the JJB Stadium against Wigan, just a week after beating them in the cup final.

The run of victories also included a 3–0 home win over Birmingham, which was a particular highlight of the season for Neville as the game marked his 500th appearance for the club, taking his place alongside seven legends (some of whom were childhood heroes): Joe Spence, Sir Bobby Charlton, Bill Foulkes, Tony Dunne, Alex Stepney, Denis Irwin and Ryan Giggs. But he still had a long way to go to overtake Charlton, who amassed an incredible 754 appearances in a Manchester United shirt. It was a big honour for him and he declared his ambition to continue playing for United. He still had the same passion for the game as when he first arrived in the senior side and with impeccable fitness levels it would take a brave man to bet against him making it to 600 or even 700 appearances.

The series of excellent wins reached match number seven with a 2–0 victory over Arsenal at Old Trafford. It always felt good to triumph over Arsenal, such was the rivalry and history between the two teams. This defeat left the Gunners' struggling to gain the fourth Champions League spot in the table, currently occupied by Tottenham. Both United and Arsenal had been written off after the 0–0 draw earlier in the season, but now both clubs, especially United, had the pundits drooling again. The United forwards were looking very sharp and Gary was feeling much happier. The negative manner in which United had been dismissed as title challengers had upset Neville; he believed success was just around the corner for the club. He also voiced his opinions on the title race, which many had declared to be over. But United's ruthless displays had opened up the debate once more. Gary was realistic about the team's slim chance of catching Chelsea and he expressed his happiness that United sowed seeds of doubt in people's minds: 'Whatever happens in the next four weeks,' he wrote in the *Times* on the eve of the Arsenal match, 'and whoever lifts the trophy, it is great to hear people talking about the championship race rather than a procession.' Even winning all their remaining games might not be enough for United, but their change of fortune had recharged Neville and his team-mates. United were also taking the chance to signal their intent for next season.

Goals from Wayne Rooney and Ji-Sung Park saw United keep up the pressure on Chelsea, but an unfortunate 0–0 draw at home to bottom club Sunderland, whose goalkeeper Kelvin Davis had an inspired afternoon, ended any realistic chance of catching the Blues. In an interview before the game, Neville had promised United would not be complacent because there was too much at stake, with the chance of closing the gap behind Chelsea to just four points. However, it was one of those days for the Red Devils and the title dream slipped a little further away.

Neville admitted that United had let their standards slip; second in the Premiership was not acceptable for a club of their stature. Although an automatic spot in the Champions League had been achieved, only top spot was good enough to keep the United management and the club's supporters happy. Neville could not believe the team had failed to score against Sunderland but, in reality, the title race was over before that goal-less draw. Ryan Giggs, who has played with Neville throughout his career, echoed his captain's sentiments. The experienced United players knew the recent lack of trophies had to be dealt with and the only way forward was for the squad to stick together through what had been a difficult patch.

United then won 2–1 away to Tottenham before a 3–0 defeat against Chelsea at Stamford Bridge sealed a second consecutive Premiership title for Jose Mourinho and his players. It was an agonising afternoon for United as, rather like Arsenal's victory at Old Trafford in the 2001–02 season, Neville and his team-mates had to witness the champions' celebrations. Worse still, Wayne Rooney suffered a metatarsal bone injury in his right foot in a challenge with defender Paulo Ferreira that saw the striker stretchered off the field. England players on both sides looked on with anxious faces as the nation's talisman exited. It was later revealed that Rooney's World Cup hopes were in jeopardy due to the broken bone and that the healing time for such an injury was usually at least six weeks, exactly the period remaining before England's World Cup began. And so the debate began as to whether or not Rooney would be fit for the tournament or whether he would even be selected in the squad – much as had been the case for David Beckham prior to the 2002 World Cup. It was a sad note on which to end the Premiership campaign.

The final two Premiership matches resulted in four points as United were left with only pride to play for. A draw with Middlesbrough represented another disappointing afternoon and, as the players left the field, Neville became involved in an argument with a United fan, who was seen to mouth 'disgrace' in Neville's direction. While the supporter's anger was surely aimed at the team rather than at Gary, it showed the level of frustration at the club as another disappointing season came to a close. As Neville explained to Sky Sports: 'We were both showing our passion for the club. He had a strong opinion and we had a disagreement. Now it is finished with. Manchester United has great fans.' A 4–0 hammering of Charlton closed the campaign and Ferguson was pleased to see Louis Saha's excellent return from injury continue and the performances of youngsters like

Giuseppe Rossi and Kieran Richardson. But despite the Carling Cup success, a muted atmosphere hung over Old Trafford.

Reflecting on the season Neville praised Jose Mourinho and the Chelsea team, but promised a more competitive challenge in the next campaign. With the Premiership already wrapped up for the Blues, he wrote in his *Times* column at the start of May: 'It is damned hard to win the championship, so I have no hesitation in congratulating Chelsea on retaining the title. They will be favourites next season, but our improvement since the turn of the year makes me believe that we can fight them all the way.' As captain, Gary expected nothing less of his team. Clearly, Chelsea's consistency had been the key factor and winning eighteen of their first twenty games had been extremely impressive. Neville was pleased with United's second half of the season but, by then, the players had left themselves with too much to do. The Blues had clearly raised the bar and it was up to United and the other challengers to match them.

He also admitted that another title triumph was imperative for him before he retired in order to feel he had gone out at the top. Having won it four times earlier in his career, he feared the latter part of his time at United would be considered a failure if he did not collect another Premiership-winners' medal. The Premiership trophy was the one the United management and players were desperate to win back. Once more it had proved beyond United in this campaign, but at least the Carling

Cup success ensured it had not been a trophy-less season. For Neville, 2006 will always be remembered as the year when he lifted his first trophy as Manchester United captain, but he and all those connected to the club knew it was Premiership and Champions League glory that United ought to be competing for.

As Neville moved on from United's failures in the Premiership and in Europe, all of the country was full of excitement about the World Cup. With Sven-Goran Eriksson having decided to step down after the tournament, the appointment of a new England manager once again rumbled on. The pressure to appoint an English manager was immense after the failures during Eriksson's spell in charge and a shortlist was formed, which included Steve McClaren, Stuart Pearce, Sam Allardyce and Alan Curbishley. Martin O'Neill was another candidate, despite the fact that he was not English. Then the job seemed to have been awarded to Luiz Felipe Scolari, only for the Brazilian to turn the post down.

Neville understood the difficult situation facing Brian Barwick, the FA's chief executive, and voiced his opinions on the managerial candidates in his column on 1 May: 'Luiz Felipe Scolari clearly gave the FA the impression that he wanted to come and who can legislate for a man withdrawing so suddenly? The FA now has the chance to get someone who really wants the job, someone who rightly regards it as one of the biggest and best in world football.' Gary had always been prepared to accept foreign managers for the job, but now he felt it was time to select an English manager, either Steve McClaren or Sam Allardyce, both of whom had impressed Neville.

On 4 May, after months of speculation, the FA eventually chose Steve McClaren to take over the post. McClaren, who had first shown his coaching skills as Ferguson's assistant at Old Trafford before his move to Middlesbrough, was familiar to Neville. The pair had worked together both at United and in the England camp and Gary had always respected McClaren's ideas.

As Neville and his team-mates headed off to Portugal with their families for a relaxing fortnight, it was a rare chance for him to catch his breath before the crucial month of World Cup football ahead. He knew it might be his last taste of World Cup action and was determined to make the most of it. In the *Times* on 15 June he wrote about his aspirations for the tournament: 'I hope for a fantastic spectacle, but most of all I long to reach the final on 9 July. I know England fans will say they have heard it all before when the players say we can win the World Cup, but this is the most technically gifted side for a long time.'

Chapter 10

Germany and the New Era

The 2006 World Cup – the last major tournament under manager Sven-Goran Eriksson – will once again be remembered as one of failure for England. Billed as potential winners, the team stuttered through the group stage and the second round without moving out of first gear, only to crash out on penalties to an ordinary Portugal side in an all-too-familiar World Cup story.

Pre-tournament, Neville stated it was time for England to fulfil their potential in the big games. He told the media: 'There can be no excuses this tournament for us. No bad decisions, no missed penalty, no poor performance. The make-or-break moments in this tournament we have to make our own. And if we don't, we'll come home and we'll be a nearly team.' He knew it could be his last World Cup and was desperate for

England to make a big impact on the competition. Just as had been the case with Beckham in 2002, all the pre-tournament attention was focused on whether Wayne Rooney's foot would heal in time and this constant speculation was not at all helpful for the other players. Eriksson had gambled on the striker's fitness by including him in the squad and the nation sat in suspense, praying that their big star would be passed fit to play. Neville acknowledged that Rooney would be a big loss if he was ruled out, but he reminded everyone that there were plenty of other stars in the team who could be match-winners for England. Neville, as he searched for positives, also suggested that Rooney's possible absence might make England less predictable in their style of play.

Gary found the tournament particularly frustrating, sitting out three of England's five games with a calf injury, but he never let it affect his morale. He accepted it was just bad luck and got on with working his way back to full fitness and enjoying the tournament. Neville is rarely comfortable when he is forced into the role of spectator. He said in the *Times* in January 1999: 'As far as United goes, I'm not a particularly good watcher of games,' and later that month he claimed 'being injured is just about the worst thing for any footballer to endure. I was the only one in the treatment-room last week, so I found myself staring out of the window and listening to the rest of the lads laughing and joking while I was feeling miserable.'

Neville appeared in England's opening match against Paraguay, a 1–0 win in the Frankfurt sun. David Beckham's free-kick, flicked into his own net by Carlos Gamarra after only three minutes, gave England the perfect start in their opening game, much to Neville's delight. The first half hour was dominated by England, but then Paraguay came into the game and Gary and his team-mates wilted. Fortunately for England, the Paraguayans had little to offer in the final third and were unable to capitalise on their intense pressure. Too much possession was wasted by England in hopeful long balls to Peter Crouch and the team ended up clinging on for the narrow win.

The lacklustre performance in the second half drew criticism from both the English media and their Paraguayan opponents. Joe Lovejoy of the *Times* wrote: 'England were anything but inspired by their early success.' While Paraguayan striker Roque Santa Cruz mocked: 'England might need it to rain if they are going to win the World Cup. England didn't really have a rhythm in their game. They will have to be better and show more rhythm and they must hope it is not as hot.' The weather, of course, had been a major factor. Games played in the 2.00 p.m. heat were never going to be as open as the evening games because of the energy-sapping high temperatures, but it should have been an incentive for England to keep possession for longer periods and make the opposition toil. Sadly, England were guilty of constantly seeking a long pass when shorter, sharper passing would have been more appropriate – the kind adopted so successfully by Andrea Pirlo and Gennaro Gattuso in Italy's World Cup-winning midfield.

Neville picked up his calf injury during training and missed the final two group games against Trinidad and Tobago and Sweden. While England picked up four points from the two matches to win the group, the quality of the performances was still poor. The Trinidad and Tobago game saw England score two late goals to salvage the win and the BBC website was far from positive about the performance. It said: 'It had looked like being a major embarrassment for England coach Sven-Goran Eriksson, with his team short on ideas and confidence. They created plenty of chances without ever being in total control of the match and can count themselves fortunate to have got out of jail.'

A brilliant strike from Joe Cole was the highlight of the 2–2 draw with Sweden, but defensive frailties and a tournament-ending injury to Michael Owen left a sour taste in the mouths of England fans. Matt Dickinson, reporting for the *Times* said: 'They could have conceded four or five goals just from set-pieces. Having lost their leading scorer, England can scarcely afford to wobble at the back.' And Kevin McCarra of the *Guardian* went further, claiming: 'The sources of the side's anxiety were all too obvious on a troubled night.' Neville's replacement Jamie Carragher was steady in these games without looking anything more than a stand-in and did not link up as effectively with Beckham. He had hoped to return for the second-round clash with Ecuador, but was unable to regain fitness in time and Owen Hargreaves stepped into the role as Eriksson curiously chose the second round of a World Cup to experiment with Michael Carrick in the holding role. Ultimately, England overcame Ecuador 1–0 to reach the World Cup quarter-finals, but it was not a game without scares. The *Times* used the headline 'England labour into last eight'; it summed up a deserved but greatly over-complicated victory.

Portugal, victors against Holland in a game of twenty-five fouls and twenty cards, were to be England's opponents in the quarter-finals, deprived of the suspended Deco and Costinha. It was a re-match of the Euro 2004 quarter-final and the talk in the media was all about England being on a revenge mission. There were suggestions that Luis Felipe Scolari had become Eriksson's nemesis, because Scolari had eliminated England from the 2002 World Cup as Brazil boss and from Euro 2004 as manager of Portugal. England hoped it would be third time lucky for Eriksson and the players.

Neville's recovery was completed in time and he and Sven-Goran Eriksson spoke out at an England press conference to emphasise his fitness. The Swede explained: 'Gary Neville did everything today. He is looking very good. As things stand, I think he will play on Saturday. His experience over many years might be very important in a game like this against Portugal. He is important to the balance of the side and it should be very good to have him back.' Gary, too, deemed himself ready, having been involved in training with the rest of the squad: 'I am confident my calf is fully fit. I have been injured the last three matches and I have not enjoyed it and I hope I will be involved on Saturday, because you don't feel part of it when injured.'

The same press conference saw Neville give a motivated and positive rallying-cry ahead of the Portugal match. Compared to some of the premeditated, robotic answers of the other players in interviews, Neville was refreshingly honest and open: 'My thoughts are all positive for Saturday. I'm thinking about the opportunity, about the importance of the occasion for the country, about how proud all of us should be to be involved in it. How many players get the opportunity to play in a World Cup quarter-final for England? Not many – we have that opportunity and we have to go and make the most of it. I believe there is a time and a moment for players to deliver. And I think it's Saturday.'

Neville promised there would be no excuses if England were eliminated by Portugal and even claimed that the team would have failed the country's supporters. It was time to fulfil their potential or face the fact that any talk of England being serious contenders was nonsense. He felt there was a limit to how many times England could feel unlucky and look to the next tournament. The team was at its peak in Germany and needed to take advantage of this opportunity, especially as the next

World Cup in South Africa would be even hotter and there were no guarantees on England receiving a generous draw for the tournament.

To be recognised as a great England team, the players had to reach a final. The time had come to prove themselves. Neville admitted the team had been handed a fortunate route thus far and felt they were capable of overcoming Portugal to book themselves a place in the semi-finals. He expressed his desire to avoid being recalled as 'a nearly team, a team that had potential but didn't deliver'. The players were two matches away from the World Cup final and Neville wanted to be remembered as a World Cup winner. He knew the team was brimming with talent and understood the excitement of the England supporters. As he explained to the press: 'There's great expectation, but expectation that I think is correct and right and we shouldn't shy away from it. We won't be coming to you on Saturday night and saying, well, 2008 could be our time. We'd said all along that 2006 was it.' It was an honest and brutal assessment of what was riding on the game ... and an acknowledgement of the desperate price of failure. It was an assessment the assembled journalists respected.

There is something very authoritative about the way Neville speaks about football. This is a quality brought out in his captaincy and the way he handles himself off the pitch. He has set beliefs and, if he is offended by an aspect of football, he will speak up. Andrew Cole, a former United and England team-mate of Neville, reveals Gary has something to say on any topic. In his autobiography *Andrew Cole*, he wrote: 'He has an opinion on anything and everything, politics, football, stocks and shares, you name it, and, if you take his word for it, he has never been wrong in his life.'

The quarter-final against Portugal, though, was a far too familiar story. The two sides looked evenly matched for over an hour before Wayne Rooney was dismissed by referee Horacio Elizondo for a stamp on Ricardo Carvalho. With only ten men, England fought bravely and repelled attack after attack from their opponents. David Beckham was forced off through injury early in the second half and, as he was substituted, he passed the captain's armband on to Neville. Gary led the side well, throwing everything into defending the England goal. Cristiano Ronaldo, Neville's United team-mate, who was at the centre of the Rooney sending-off, gave him a tough time in the first half, but Neville grew in stature as the game went on. No goals in extra-time led to the dreaded penalty shootout and the painful 3–1 defeat that sent England home as Frank Lampard, Steven Gerrard and Jamie Carragher all had their penalties saved by Portugal goalkeeper Ricardo, the man who had been the hero of the Euro 2004 shootout.

Sven-Goran Eriksson's reign as England manager came to an end after the World Cup shootout loss to Portugal. It is likely that his involvement with the national team will be remembered in a negative light, but few of the players he has worked with have anything bad to say against him. Towards the end of his spell as manager, the anti-Eriksson feeling swamped the back pages and his controversial squad selection – including teenager Theo Walcott, untried in the Premiership, as one of only four strikers – was heavily criticised. The whole World Cup campaign brought widespread bitterness to the entire country.

However, it was certainly time to bring in a new manager with a fresh approach – the fifth manager of Neville's international career. Indeed, Neville's continued involvement with the national team is a testament to his attitude and consistency. Of the players in the 2006 World Cup squad, Gary and Sol Campbell were the only two survivors from Terry Venables' Euro '96 squad and Neville was the only player to have made the starting XI. He has made the right-back position his own through his ten years in the team and it is one area in which there is rarely any debate over selection.

There was a feeling, though, that England had really missed a trick over the past few international tournaments. Portugal and Germany, two nearby host nations, were ideal locations for mounting successful tournament bids. Many factors were in England's favour, including the minimal time required to adapt and the more comfortable temperatures – admittedly the early-afternoon kick-offs were very hot, but they were preferable to the scorching heat of Japan and Korea in 2002 and the likely temperatures in South Africa in 2010. The players were able to have their wives and girlfriends with them in Germany and a number of the squad had played club games in European competitions in Portugal and Germany.

Looking back to how motivated and confident Neville was in his press conference, the pain of the quarter-final elimination will surely stay with him for a long time. Not only the cruel nature of losing a penalty shootout, but also because he and the team really believed that this was their chance. The aftermath of the team's elimination was the sorry saga of Eriksson's departure. The media sent out mocking headlines, giving the Swede a sad exit, but it was undeniable that England had fallen short of their potential under Eriksson's management.

*****

The summer of 2006 was a painful one for everyone connected with the England national team, but Neville returned to United raring to go and was determined to lift some silverware at the end of the campaign. United's poor showings in the Premiership had gone on for too long and Gary was running out of chances to restore the club to the top of the domestic game.

The Carling Cup win had given him the taste of captaining a winning team and he wanted to build on that with Premiership and Champions League glory.

There were many rumours flying around during pre-season, linking United with a number of top-class players. Ferguson seemed certain to target the central midfield position in a bid to find a long-term replacement for Roy Keane. Though John O'Shea and Darren Fletcher had been useful fill-ins, there was no doubt among United supporters that a couple of fresh midfielders would spice up the core of the side. Neville was able to welcome Paul Scholes back into the side again after the diminutive midfielder had overcome the eye problems that had kept him out of much of the previous campaign. A fully fit Scholes was like a new signing for United and, with Ole Gunnar Solskjaer and Alan Smith also coming back from injury, the squad suddenly seemed a lot stronger.

In the end, despite rumours linking the club with Argentine Javier Mascherano and Frenchman Mahamadou Diarra, Sir Alex Ferguson turned to Neville's England colleague Michael Carrick as the answer to the midfield problem and paid Tottenham £18.6 million for his services. Ferguson also brought in Tomasz Kuszczak as a back-up goalkeeper for Edwin van der Sar. Kuszczak had Premiership experience from his time at West Brom and the United manager was keen to be able to turn to this know-how if van der Sar was unavailable, rather than to an untried youngster.

Chelsea continued to show they were a fully established financial powerhouse. The Blues splashed out £31 million on Ukrainian striker Andriy Shevchenko from Italian giants AC Milan to give them extra firepower for the Champions League. Michael Ballack, another player with European experience, also joined

Chelsea under the Bosman ruling from Bayern Munich. It made United's summer transfer activity look pretty minimal in comparison, but Neville and his team-mates approached the new season full of belief. Eager to stand up to their rivals, Gary could not resist a dig at Chelsea, claiming that United were still one of the best clubs in the world for producing young talent and that the Blues could never emulate them, however much money they spent. It was only a minor issue, but it was encouraging for all United fans to hear the club captain sounding as though he was ready for a fierce title battle.

In the end, a bigger name exited Old Trafford than any of those who arrived. After years of excellent service, Dutch striker Ruud van Nistelrooy left United for Real Madrid in a deal reported to be worth £10.3 million. His last few months at the club had been difficult, with rumours suggesting he and Cristiano Ronaldo had fallen out and, as a consequence, upset Sir Alex Ferguson. In the end, the move suited both parties and the United fans had to say goodbye to one of the club's most lethal goalscorers. Since his arrival at Old Trafford in 2001, van Nistelrooy racked up 150 goals in 219 appearances. Ferguson's decision to leave van Nistelrooy on the bench during the latter part of the campaign had largely been influenced by the return to fitness of Louis Saha. Saha, who had suffered several injury setbacks at the club, showed enough promise in the last few games of the season to convince Ferguson that he could afford to allow van Nistelrooy to leave.

For Neville, there was the excitement of his first full season as captain of the club and he led the side out at Old Trafford on the opening day against Fulham. United hammered the London club 5–1 to make an impressive start with Wayne Rooney scoring twice. Neville was taken off at half-time to rest his calf, as there was no need to risk him with the game already well under control. The team continued to play attractive, attacking football and Charlton were the next team to suffer. United won 3–0 at The Valley and Solskjaer was among the scorers, marking his return to the big time after his injury nightmares. A third win away to Watford brought more praise for the way the team had started the season, with Ryan Giggs scoring the winning goal. Neville sat out the games against Charlton and Watford in an attempt to clear up his calf injury.

*****

England were handed a kind qualifying group for Euro 2008 in Austria and Switzerland. They were drawn in Group E with Andorra, Croatia, Estonia, Israel, FYR Macedonia and Russia. The teams to watch out for were Israel, Croatia and Russia, but all of them were thought to be very beatable opponents and the nation expected top spot to be clinched without any problems. Looking at other groups England had certainly been very fortunate. France and Italy, the 2006 World Cup finalists, had both been drawn in the same group as

Scotland along with World Cup quarter-finalists Ukraine. Wales' group boasted the power of Germany and the Czech Republic, giving Ryan Giggs little chance of finally appearing at a major international tournament – one of football's biggest travesties.

Steve McClaren's spell in charge of the national team began in convincing fashion. There were a number of skeptics over the appointment of McClaren, largely due to his connection with the unsuccessful Eriksson era, but a 4–0 win over Greece in his first game in charge led to widespread praise of the way the team had played. It was admittedly only a friendly against a team that had not even qualified for the 2006 World Cup, but it was a solid display nonetheless.

McClaren had immediately stamped his own impression on the England team. He made the massive decision to drop David Beckham from the squad and gave Phil Neville a recall to the side. Beckham had resigned as captain of the national team after the 2006 World Cup, giving an emotional speech, and McClaren decided he no longer deserved to be a part of the international set-up. Gary felt for Beckham, who seemed to have taken all the blame for England's poor showing in Germany. As always, Beckham consulted with Neville and it was a testing time for Gary as he had to put his own excitement about the new era to one side in order to console his best friend on his exclusion from the squad.

This left the new boss with a big decision to make over

the new England captain. Three leading candidates emerged – John Terry of Chelsea, Steven Gerrard of Liverpool and Neville. It was a great honour for Gary to be linked with the captaincy and it was a tribute to the way he had begun his spell as United skipper. In the end, McClaren chose John Terry to lead the side, but Neville and the rest of the squad were happy with the manager's selection. Terry had proven himself and was a highly respected player. After all, Terry and Steven Gerrard had both been captain of their respective clubs far longer than Neville; the United skipper could hardly complain about being overlooked. It is likely, though, that McClaren gave Neville's case for the captaincy due consideration, having worked with him for many years and being a huge admirer of Gary's all-round ability. Indeed, both Alan Ball and Jimmy Armfield felt that Neville should take the captain's armband ahead of England's first qualifying match. Gary would definitely have loved to have been named as the new captain, but leading out his country is of the few childhood ambitions it seems he will not achieve.

The first Euro 2008 qualifiers saw England facing Andorra and FYR Macedonia. Again the opposition was extremely weak, but the right results were achieved. Andorra were hammered 5–0 at Old Trafford and FYR Macedonia were beaten 1–0. Gary missed both these games due to a groin injury, but his frustration will have been eased by the fact that his brother Phil was moved into the starting line-up to replace him. Phil had failed to make Eriksson's World Cup squad, but McClaren, who had worked with both Nevilles at United for many years, knew he was a worthy member of the squad. Phil's versatility makes him a very useful player and his early season form for Everton – wearing the captain's armband – was excellent. It was pleasing for the Neville family not only to see both brothers involved in the international set-up again but also to witness both captaining their respective clubs in Premiership action.

*****

Gary's return to action came against Tottenham in United's fourth game of the campaign. In front of expectant United fans at Old Trafford, Neville captained United to a fourth consecutive win thanks to Ryan Giggs' first-half goal. The crowd of 75,434 was a new Premiership record attendance and Sky Sports named Neville Man of the Match for his tireless running on the right flank. However, Tottenham wasted several good opportunities to take a share of the points. Gary admitted as much in a post-match interview: 'We're just happy to get away with the win.'

After the game, Neville refused to get carried away by the team's impressive start to the season. Having spent so many years at the top, he expressed his delight at recording four wins out of four, but would not be drawn into any title predictions. He knew there was a long way to go and that it was far too early to judge whether the team would be genuine challengers for the Premiership trophy. He also explained how the players and the management had discussed the importance of making a good start to the campaign, especially considering the disappointing early performances of previous seasons. Neville wisely said that the team's biggest tests were yet to come.

United had been without Paul Scholes and Wayne Rooney for the matches against Charlton, Watford and Tottenham due to suspension. The pair were sent off in the LG Amsterdam Tournament during pre-season and the FA refused to overturn their bans. United felt massively aggrieved and Neville was particularly unhappy with the FA verdict. Speaking to the media, he said: 'It is a shocking decision, absolutely shocking. But what do you expect? I certainly didn't expect anything else. We don't look after our own in this country.' The suspensions certainly seemed harsh considering that the red cards did not even come in a competitive match.

Not only was it crucial for the team to improve in the Premiership but also in the Champions League where their efforts had been well below par in the past two seasons. The second-round exit against Porto in 2004 had been bad enough, but failing to qualify from the group stage in 2005 was a huge embarrassment for the club and it left the players needing to prove themselves again in Europe. For Neville, who savours the big European nights, missing out on qualification was a harsh blow and the players began their campaign full of confidence and desperate to make amends. Celtic were

United's opponents in the first game of the group stage and the animosity between Sir Alex Ferguson and Celtic boss Gordon Strachan dominated the pre-match build-up. In a very open, entertaining game, United emerged with a 3–2 victory and three points thanks to Ole Gunnar Solskjaer's winner. The only disappointment on the night was the injury to Ryan Giggs, who limped off with a hamstring injury – it has been a persistent problem for him throughout his career.

Neville had identified the matches against Celtic and then Arsenal as the real tests of United's form and the team had dug deep to past the first test. The Gunners awaited the following weekend, on the same day Liverpool travelled to Stamford Bridge to face the champions, Chelsea. In a poor afternoon for United that never saw them produce their best football, they lost to a late goal from Emmanuel Adebayor. It was a huge disappointment after what had been such a solid start to the season. Neville was defiant after the match and claimed the defeat would fire United up for the remainder of the campaign. The rivalry with Arsenal, so fierce in previous years, had become less heated, with neither team consistently challenging Chelsea for the title. However, the defeat to the Gunners was still hugely painful and the players knew a big response was required.

A match against newly promoted Reading seemed like a good opportunity to return to winning ways, but the Royals fought hard and deserved a 1–1 draw. Reading took the lead through a Kevin Doyle penalty, harshly awarded for a handball by Neville. It seemed far from clear-cut, but the spot-kick was awarded and United needed an equaliser from Cristiano Ronaldo to head back to Manchester with a point. It was not the result United had hoped for, but the players had fought back well after Reading's goal.

Mention of Benfica brings several United European moments to mind. The glorious night in 1968 is one but, most recently, it was Benfica who had eliminated United from the Champions League the previous season. Revenge was very much on the agenda for Neville and his team-mates as they headed to Portugal, hoping to make it six points out of six in the group. In some quarters, the club's European pedigree was starting to be doubted and a strong campaign in the Champions League was essential. United again failed to find their best form against Benfica, but they had the experience to hang on for a 1–0 win. It was the kind of game the team had thrown away the previous season, but the encouragement came from the fact the players seemed to have learned from the experience. It was a valuable three points. Neville marshalled the defence superbly and United's stubborn display was rewarded with Louis Saha's fantastic strike from the edge of the area.

The team returned to winning ways in the Premiership at Old Trafford against Newcastle with two goals from the rejuvenated Solskjaer. Hugely popular at the club, the Norwegian striker was repaying the loyalty and patience Sir Alex Ferguson had shown him throughout his long lay-off. With Ryan Giggs and Alan Smith regaining full fitness, United's pursuit of the title was looking promising and the depth of the squad seemed capable of matching their title challengers. Chelsea's start to the season had been very similar to United's. After seven games, both teams had recorded five wins, one draw and one defeat. Arsenal and Liverpool had both made stuttering starts, but it seemed that Chelsea would not be running away with the Premiership this season. The level of consistency, though, needed to be higher than had been the case the previous season for United, when too many points had been thrown away against lesser sides and when Old Trafford appeared to have become less of a fortress.

Perhaps the biggest highlight of the early-season matches for United was the form of Cristiano Ronaldo. After his involvement in Wayne Rooney's red card at the World Cup, it seemed that Ronaldo would face a torrid season and might even leave United, with Real Madrid poised to swoop for the winger. But in response to the abuse he received at away grounds, he produced some scintillating displays of attacking football, creating and scoring important goals. Gary linked up well with him and the pair always looked dangerous down the right flank. It looked as though the partnership could prove as effective as the Neville-Beckham partnership had been in United's golden era of the late nineties.

Nobody at the club was getting carried away, though. The quality of their rivals was such that United needed to stay fully focused. Chelsea's new signings were taking time to settle in, but few doubted that Jose Mourinho's team would be in contention and hard to stop. But Neville had seen United fall as many as ten or twelve points behind the leaders before the New Year. The feeling at Old Trafford was that if the team could keep pace with Chelsea, they would have the nerve to make it count in the closing stages of the campaign.

*****

Following their 100 per cent start to the Euro 2008 qualification campaign, the third qualifier, the return game against FYR Macedonia, saw McClaren contemplate a switch from the 4-4-2 formation he had adopted for the previous three matches in favour of 3-5-2. Some claimed the players were influencing the tactics; it was a claim Neville strongly denied. He has been part of the England set-up for over a decade and so was well-placed to judge the situation. He said: 'Regarding people saying we will influence what system we will play, that isn't happening – and hasn't happened. I don't understand where that has come from.' Pre-match, Neville called for the team to perform together to continue their winning start to the McClaren era. With Wembley taking shape he knew it was likely to be the last competitive game England would play at Old Trafford and he acknowledged it had been a good ground for England, with the team having won all of the eight games played there before the FYR Macedonia match. Despite winning his eighty-third cap in the Macedonia clash, Neville insisted that only tournament glory would provide a fitting end to his international career. He told the media: 'Ultimately, you are judged on whether you win things. Being part of a winning team makes the individual and, unless I do that, I won't have had a successful England career. The greatest players for me are the ones who played in the great winning teams.' He acknowledged that his tally of caps was impressive, but he knew that team glory was more important than personal records.

McClaren eventually opted to stick with the 4-4-2 formation and the team came out with all guns blazing against their Macedonian opponents. There was plenty of space for Neville to roam into down the right flank and he exploited it with several surging runs forward. With the game still goal-less, Neville had a fantastic opportunity to break the deadlock after the goalkeeper had parried out Peter Crouch's header, but his shot missed the target. The match finished 0–0 and the media slammed England's poor display; their opponents had outclassed them for large patches of the game. Qualifying matches against teams like FYR Macedonia are no-win situations for managers. The expectation of a resounding victory is so high that only a four- or five-goal margin is considered acceptable. It ends up putting more pressure on the players. The 0–0 draw certainly was unacceptable, though, and Neville knew the performance needed to be much better in their next match the following Wednesday against Croatia. It was a game that suddenly took on a far greater significance: Neville and his team-mates wanted to make amends for the poor display against Macedonia.

The build-up to this latest qualifier was dominated by speculation over Wayne Rooney's loss of form. The draw with Macedonia had brought a lot of criticism and Rooney had been the scapegoat. Neville was unhappy with the media's treatment of the young star and insisted the team were not concerned about the youngster's form. Looking back to the weekend, he told the media: 'There wasn't a lot of space for Wayne and not a lot of service he would have liked. But that will come. We need to improve on that for Wednesday and get better service into the front players. With better service, Wayne will do well.' Everyone hoped he would soon start producing the performances that had marked him out as such a star.

This time, in Croatia, McClaren did opt to use the 3-5-2 formation, but with disastrous consequences. Neville played as right wing-back, but the position was not as comfortable for him as the right-back slot. The whole England performance was well below par and Croatia took the lead just after half-time. The second goal was calamitous. Neville played a routine backpass to Paul Robinson, but the ball bobbled just in front of the goalkeeper, bounced over Robinson's kicking foot and rolled into the net. It went down as a Neville own goal; in reality it was a freak incident. Gary had finally scored for England, but nobody was laughing. Henry Winter described Gary's 'goal' as 'an innocuous pass back' and nobody blamed him for the outcome. It was just one of those nights for Neville and England. McClaren faced up to the criticism of the new formation, telling the media: 'It was my decision to change and we lost the game, so it's my responsibility. I have to accept that criticism. I pick the players and I pick the system.'

*****

United continued their excellent start to the Premiership campaign, keeping their noses ahead of Chelsea at the top of the table. A tricky away game against Wigan was next on United's schedule. Their opponents had enjoyed an impressive run the previous season and took an early lead here. But this United side had a lot of character and, although Gary was absent, the passion of the players still embodied everything about United. Ryan Giggs came on for the second half as Sir Alex Ferguson switched to 4-4-2 and gave Wayne Rooney the space to threaten Wigan. It was a masterstroke and United fought back to win 3–1. It was the type of game United had surrendered in previous seasons so Neville would have been proud of the way the team refused to give in.

Gary's injury problems also kept him out of the midweek game in the Champions League against FC Copenhagen. It was frustrating for him to be missing so many games in his first full season as captain but, as ever, he simply got on with his football and worked hard to regain full fitness. FC Copenhagen were brushed aside easily at Old Trafford. The Danes had been surprise qualifiers from the preliminary rounds of the competition and goals from Paul Scholes, John O'Shea and Kieran Richardson gave the team a solid 3–0 win.

The next test for United came in the form of Liverpool, who had endured a poor start to the season. There was no chance of Neville missing out on this game and it was inevitable he would be fit enough to return to the starting line-up. Once again, Liverpool suffered a disappointing afternoon as United powered past them, winning 2–0. Gary put in a very calm, steady performance, while his fellow youth-team colleagues Paul Scholes and Ryan Giggs also performed excellently to show that the United core of old was still going strong. It was a special occasion for Scholes and Wayne Rooney, who both reached personal milestones. For Scholes it was his 500th appearance for United, while Rooney was playing in his 100th career game. Neville has never had anything but compliments for the pair and it is players like Scholes and Rooney whom Gary is so proud to lead out as captain. He was delighted to welcome Paul Scholes into the 500-appearance club; he was the third Fergie Fledgling to reach the landmark. This underlines the incredible work of Eric Harrison and, of course, Ferguson himself in bringing through a group of players of which three would make over 500 appearances for United.

Wayne Rooney continued to endure much criticism for his performances during the season. He had scored twice in United's opening-day win against Fulham, but had failed to register a goal since and his displays for England had been below par. But Neville knew that opponents would soon be paying the price; Rooney was destined to return to his best. Poor Bolton were the first to witness a back-in-form Rooney as he slammed in a brilliant hat-trick at the Reebok Stadium. United had seen Chelsea win earlier in the day and set about Bolton, determined to return to the top of the Premiership table. Neville, back in the side, was thrilled for Rooney and was equally delighted with the way United had destroyed a very good Bolton team.

Having taken nine points out of nine thus far in the Champions League, Neville knew that victory away to FC Copenhagen would guarantee qualification and the players were desperate to clinch qualification in top spot. Gary's injury problems again caused him to sit out and, with Ryan Giggs and Louis Saha also carrying niggles, Sir Alex Ferguson had to shuffle the pack slightly with his selection. If Benfica failed to beat Celtic in the other fixture in the group, then a draw for United would be enough to seal qualification. The game in Copenhagen represented a chance for the team to banish the memories of the previous season and book their place in the second-round draw. But it was a bad night for United as they wasted numerous golden chances and lost 1–0 to a sucker punch from Marcus Allback, the former Aston Villa striker. Confirmation of their qualification for the next phase of the Champions League would have to wait.

United collected another emphatic three points in the Premiership with a 3–0 win against an under-strength Portsmouth. Neville put in a fantastic performance, storming forward down the right flank and going close to scoring on several occasions. Hard as he tries, he still lacks the composure to take advantage of some of the promising positions he finds himself in, but then he is not paid to be a goalscorer. He received glowing praise from the *Independent on Sunday*, which selected him as the Man of the Match. Journalist Steve Tongue wrote: 'One of Sir Alex Ferguson's most loyal servants was dominant on his manager's big day and deserved a goal to round it off.' The clean sheet was United's sixth in the Premiership and their eighth in all competitions, which represented a very solid start.

The day was a memorable one for Sir Alex Ferguson as he celebrated his twentieth anniversary as Manchester United manager. It is an outstanding achievement and has cemented his place among the great managers of all time. Neville delivered a fitting tribute to the media about the man who has been his boss ever since his debut in 1992, claiming that nobody expected Sir Matt Busby's records to be beaten, but that Ferguson had done just that, and that the pair were responsible for putting United in such a lofty position in English football. He added that Ferguson had taken the club back to the level where it belonged. Having gone twenty-six years without winning the title, he put United back on track to win championships, FA Cups and even the Champions League.

On a more personal level, Ferguson had proved the perfect father figure, especially with the fledglings of Neville's year. This is something that Gary will always treasure. He said: 'As a young player you're wary of him and even now when he walks in the room everybody goes a bit quiet. But if you're in trouble, his is the door you knock on. You might have something going on in your personal life and he'll listen. That's where he wins respect. People looking in from the outside might think he has got performances from players over the years through fear, but it's more than that.' There will never be another Alex Ferguson. His super-human efforts at Old Trafford are seemingly impossible to replicate, particularly as he achieved so much with so many homegrown players. The chances of Chelsea, Arsenal and Liverpool doing this in the future seem remote, as all three clubs have looked to the transfer market more eagerly than their youth teams. Ryan Giggs, too, has very fond memories of Sir Alex Ferguson's time at Old Trafford. It is interesting to note that 2007 will mark Giggs' twentieth year at the club; his journey to the top at United has coincided almost directly with Ferguson's.

The United manager was thrilled with the performance to mark his twentieth anniversary at the club. He reflected on his spell in charge as amazing, but he could not believe that the twenty years had passed so quickly. Ferguson reserved special praise, on what was a special day for Neville, Scholes and Giggs: 'They're great players and if we're in a challenging position next April these are the players who've been there before and I think they'll get us through.'

Rather than dwell on the past, though, there was a Premiership title to compete for. Chelsea's 2–1 defeat against Tottenham at White Hart Lane the same weekend provided Ferguson with an additional gift to celebrate his anniversary as United moved three points clear of the Blues at the top of the table. Neville was already looking ahead to the huge clash with Chelsea at Old Trafford on 26 November. Even at that early stage, there was no doubt it would have a huge impact on the outcome of the Premiership title race and there would be plenty of psychological points to be scored. United proved in the same fixture the previous season that they could still conquer the Blues and arguably the Red Devils had made a more impressive start to the Premiership season, playing flowing, attacking football. With several United youngsters impressing as the team progressed in the Carling Cup, Neville was happy to see the club competing for four trophies. It made a big change from the previous season when, after ten league games, Chelsea had already built a double-figure lead over United.

With several more qualifiers and then Euro 2008 ahead, Neville is hopeful of extending his international career long enough to win his 100th cap for his country. Having been a regular member of the England side since his debut in 1995, Neville's consistent performances have allowed him to become a mainstay of the team and have ensured that he has outlasted all the other first-team players from the Euro '96 squad. It is an exceptional achievement and should not be underestimated. Only Peter Shilton, Bobby Moore, Bobby Charlton and Billy Wright have passed the 100-cap mark and so Gary would be entering a truly elite group of footballers. Time is on his side and there is every reason to think he will reach the milestone.

There is no sign of Neville's England career coming to an end. His form and fitness should enable him to spend many more years at the top. He looks to be a certainty for the 2008 European Championships and it is possible that he can make it to South Africa in 2010 for one last go at winning the World Cup. The words of football great Sir Tom Finney will have provided Neville with even more confidence. Finney, speaking to the *Manchester Evening News*, gave a glowing assessment of Neville's qualities: 'He is a very tidy and busy player who always impresses me. England need players with his attitude. He's a winner. I like what I see in him – he's a fine and very mobile defender who reads the game well. He is a brave, unsung hero.' For Finney, Gary never let the team down and always worked hard. While he could hardly be termed a match-winner, Finney believed he was invaluable to the side with his whole-hearted commitment. As a former winger, it was high praise indeed for Finney to say that he would not have enjoyed facing the Manchester United player.

Chapter 11

Retirement

When Neville does take a step back from football, he will have the chance to enjoy some of the relaxation he has missed out on during his career. Ever since his teenage years, Gary has devoted himself to his profession and his daily routine has always been football-orientated, despite having a variety of other interests. He is an exceptionally hard-working professional, often doing extra training to work on his game, and he thrives on the company of his team-mates, so it will be particularly hard for him to adjust to a life away from the pitch. The camaraderie with his team-mates, the magical on-field moments and the rewarding feeling of running out in front of a sell-out crowd will be impossible to replace. But his retirement will allow him to savour several things close to his heart, such as playing golf and spending time in Malta – both of which are restricted by his United and England commitments. Most importantly, he will be able to devote more time to his fiancée Emma Hadfield.

The pair have been an item for several years and Neville recently asked Emma to marry him during a holiday in Malta – a second home to Gary, who owns a house there. The relationship has been kept relatively private – as is Gary's nature – except for the very public dispute with the *News of the World* newspaper. The tabloid had claimed that Ms Hadfield was having an affair while Gary was away on international duty. Emma, a former shop assistant, was extremely upset by the suggestions, which had absolutely no substance to them. She contested the allegation and the newspaper paid her £75,000 in damages. It was a difficult time for Neville: the media had interfered in his private life and this was the only occasion when the pair has found themselves in the spotlight.

Having a stable relationship is an important part of settling down for any player. It provides a base and a refuge and friends say the couple are perfect for each other. Sir Alex Ferguson had always hoped his players would be in relationships because it led to them settling down and, subsequently, to a greater devotion to their football. With so many players spending their spare time out at nightclubs, bars and all-night parties, footballers in family set-ups are always popular with managers. It tends to be a guarantee of a balanced lifestyle and, while

Gary had never been a wild youngster, Ferguson would have been pleased that his full-back had finally decided to tie the knot.

Emma, twenty-six, and Neville met in early 2004 and had been together for eighteen months when Gary popped the question. During the World Cup in Germany, Emma was spotted looking for a diamond ring to go with her engagement ring. The life of a 'WAG' (an acronym for 'wives and girlfriends') has been well documented over the past few years, probably ever since David Beckham and Victoria Adams first announced their relationship. The 'WAGs' came to the nation's attention at the 2006 World Cup, as a number of the England players' partners hit the headlines for their extravagant spending and drinking in Germany. Emma does not fit this description at all, preferring a quieter life, and this makes her a perfect match for Neville, who has admitted his dislike for nightclubs. She went to Germany to support Gary and that is what she focused her time on.

The other love in Gary's life is Malta. When he has time to spare, Neville will no doubt look to escape to the island, a place that has been special for him for many years. It has had a place in Neville's heart ever since his trips there with the United youth teams and Gary has become heavily involved in a scheme to increase Malta's popularity. In 2001, he took on the position of official tourism ambassador for Malta and was involved in promoting the holiday destination in the United

Kingdom, specialising in the Manchester area. In June 2003, Gary signed a two-year extension to his deal with the Malta Tourism Authority (MTA) and Air Malta. The MTA chief executive officer Mr Leslie Vella was delighted Gary would be offering his support for a further two years and called Neville 'a definite crowd-puller' and someone that 'people admire and look up to'. In exchange for all the work he does, the MTA and Air Malta sponsor the Gary Neville Soccer School he has set up in Malta and at which he teaches the youngsters every summer. It is a deal that works in both parties' interests and will guarantee Neville's involvement there for many years to come. He visits the islands regularly and has now bought a property there too in the fishing village of St Julians, which has undergone much development, changing it from its quiet and peaceful origins. Footballers often have their own favourite summer get-away places and Malta is where Gary goes to get away from the pressures and attention of life at United.

Another of Neville's favourite retreats is the golf course and there is no doubt that when Neville has the freedom of retirement, he will be found regularly with his bag of clubs. Golf has become somewhat of a common hobby for professional footballers and Gary is no different. With the spare time available to footballers, it has grown popular as a way to socialise off the pitch. He had always played golf with his youth-team colleagues and it is certainly a good way of bonding as a group. Neville speaks with great enthusiasm when discussing his beginnings in golf and he told Phil Yates of the *Times*: 'I love the game and it all started when I was a kid. I bought a single club from a local sports shop when I was nine, began hitting balls around on a field near my house and I was hooked.'

Gary would love to be able to play more often, but the demands of the football season rarely allow him much time to fit in a round of golf. The Old Trafford management have banned the squad from playing golf within three days of a match and it is a rule that Neville takes very seriously, despite the fact he feels it is a perfectly acceptable past-time. He does not see the harm in a few rounds of golf during the week. It is a relaxing way to spend a day off and it allows players to escape the media spotlight. Considering that some professional footballers prefer to go out drinking and gambling, golf is seemingly the kind of activity that managers would be happy for their squad to indulge in. Neville admits that normally the players do not even use up energy walking the course, preferring to hire golf buggies instead, but Sir Alex Ferguson has made it abundantly clear that he is less than keen on his players heading to the golf course. Neville explains in *For Club and Country* that Ferguson banned the team from playing golf for the last three months of the 1996–97 season because he felt it was having a bad effect on the players. It seems the manager blamed golf for a string of injuries. Just as he had banned Neville from playing cricket, Ferguson was also quick to clamp down on his golf.

Golf has brought Neville some particularly memorable moments, such as going round Rossendale [in Lancashire] in one over par. During the summer, when he has free time, he tends to enjoy fitting in a round of golf and the more he concentrates on his all-round game, the more he notices encouraging signs of improvement. He described a long drive as his favourite shot and has proved capable of hitting the ball an impressive distance, especially considering his relatively small stature. Gary also revealed that, despite the countless games of cricket and football he and Phil have played together, golf is the sport where the biggest sibling rivalry simmers. He claims he is the winner more often than Phil; it is certainly a hobby he takes very seriously. Gary often joins his England team-mates on the greens during international breaks. He tells many stories of games of golf while on England duty, including Pro-Am days and rounds against Glenn Hoddle, with money at stake. He will be itching to take advantage of the extra free-time when he ends his football career. His love for snooker, too, will probably be strengthened in retirement as he finally gets the chance to unwind.

It is also possible he will revive his interest in cricket. He still follows the sport keenly and has been seen several times at the Old Trafford cricket ground watching England Test matches. The success of the English cricket team after winning the Ashes in 2005 has raised the status of the game in the country and Neville was among the millions of crazed fans watching on as

Kevin Pietersen's hundred on the final day at The Oval secured the series win. Having seen the victory parades for the triumphant England rugby team and then the celebrations for the Ashes success, it made Neville even more desperate to bring home some silverware from an international tournament and to experience the frenzied double-decker bus ride through streets filled with people. Undoubtedly, if England brought home the World Cup or the European Championship trophy, the hysteria on the streets of London would trump anything seen during the rugby and cricket celebrations.

But he is certainly not bitter about it. He is proud to be English and was cheering as loudly as anyone when Jonny Wilkinson struck the famous drop-goal and Pietersen performed his heroics. It will also have given him great satisfaction to see a local Lancashire lad, Andrew Flintoff – who played alongside Phil in youth cricket – shining as the star performer in the series. With Lancashire currently boasting an exciting county team, Gary will enjoy going to watch his local county. His playing days contained numerous fond memories and, if he fancied putting on his whites again, no doubt Greenmount Cricket Club would welcome him back.

But the chances of Neville finishing his playing career and stepping away from the game are very slim. It seems improbable that he will go into retirement the moment he hangs up his boots, preferring to try his hand at management before sampling life without any involvement in football. He has been widely tipped as a manager for the future and has already embarked on the process of obtaining his coaching badges. Neville took part in a training course with Phil, Roy Keane and Ryan Giggs among others and it gave him a taster of what was expected of him as a coach. He is such a detailed and experienced thinker about the game that it would be a waste if he did not continue his involvement in the sport.

Neville, already a Professional Footballers' Association (PFA) representative, has been heavily involved in negotiating with the FA throughout his time as an international footballer. He would undoubtedly do a good job for the FA after he has retired but, with his clever thinking and passion, management seems the more likely option. A move into the media is not out of the question, though. He has received some excellent reviews for appearances as part of the studio panel on Sky Sports and his ability to express his thoughts clearly makes him highly suitable for such a role. Again, though, it is harder to picture Gary in an office or a studio than it is to think of him organising his players from the touchline in much the same way he instructs his fellow defenders.

He has shown great leadership skills throughout his career, convincing Sir Alex Ferguson that he was the man to take over the United captaincy when Roy Keane departed. Ferguson not only rates Neville as a great captain, he also sees Gary following him into management. He picked out Neville, Roy Keane and Ole Gunnar Solskjaer as the players most likely to embark on managerial careers once they hang up their playing boots, telling the media: 'Roy's leadership qualities are there for all to see. I think he has certainly got the qualifications and the determination to become a manager. Gary has that too, and Ole will make a great coach I am sure.' Neville's ex-United team-mate Bryan Robson, who has been a Premiership manager himself, saw management potential in Gary as well as Roy Keane: 'You look at Gary Neville and he is a strong character and it is the same with Roy. They have the drive that is needed.' This is high praise from two managers who know what it takes to make it in football management. Both men have worked with Neville and it is a tribute to Gary's character that they are so quick to praise his suitability for a managerial career.

Gary has always enjoyed taking on extra responsibility within football, from PFA positions to captaining the side. When Neville first entered the first team, Brian McClair was the PFA representative and Gary voiced his own desire to perform such a role in future years. He has always involved himself with helping the youngsters with contract negotiations at the club and always makes himself available for support and advice. He is more than happy to assist the younger players, because he recalls the support he received from the experienced professionals when he arrived in the first team and the reassuring effect their words had on him. Having spent twelve years as a regular in the United side and over a decade playing for England, there is very little in football that Neville has not seen or experienced. Indeed, at thirty-one, he is the oldest player in Steve McClaren's England squad, providing the last link with the national team at Euro '96. He has a wealth of knowledge about the game and is good-natured enough to want to pass on this wisdom to the next generation of United stars.

In retirement, every aspect of Neville's life will be less strenuously monitored. Much as he will miss the camaraderie of his team-mates and the excitement ahead of match days, there will still be plenty of positives. One thing he will not miss will be the way he has had to pay close attention to what he eats and drinks. He will be able to enjoy his food again, not worrying about straying from the strict diets imposed on players. He told the *Sun* in early March 2005 how he craves junk food at times, but has to resist temptation: 'There is a point just before matches when the smell of burgers and chips wafts down from the stands. You go down the tunnel to warm up and see a kid eating a burger ... and you think "I could just eat one of those".' He claims that while he obeys the strict diet guidelines before the game, he makes up for it afterwards by tucking into plenty of post-match food.

The healthiness of pre-match meals has gradually improved during Neville's time at the club. When he was first playing regularly for the first team, the options were very different. At eighteen, he had would have soup as a starter followed by chicken, beans and mashed potato. This was in the days of the potent drinking circles and it was incredible that the team proved so successful, despite the players' unhealthy eating and drinking at times. The type of drinking binge some of that United squad enjoyed then would never be tolerated nowadays. After trying spaghetti, fish, cereal and toast, he has now become accustomed to pre-game meals of rice and peas. It is hardly an appealing pre-match meal, but it is supposedly an effective way to prepare for a football game, as footballers today are instructed to have a diet of high-energy, low-fat food prior to matches.

Everyone connected with Manchester United will hope Neville can continue to produce his consistent form for several more years. If anything, he seems to be improving rather than deteriorating. The captaincy has given him an extra boost at exactly the right time in his career and Sir Alex Ferguson and the United supporters are reaping the benefits. Gary's main worry is the persistence of niggling injuries that have kept him out of a few games during the 2006–07 season. Having suffered with groin and calf problems, it is important he returns to full fitness and allows his injuries to heal properly. Ferguson, always tuned in to the needs of his players, will make sure Neville does not take on too much, too soon.

It has become increasingly noticeable over recent years that, since the likes of Eric Cantona, Peter Schmeichel and Roy Keane have left Old Trafford, Neville has emerged as the new hate figure at the club for opposition supporters. There is plenty of negative feeling throughout the nation towards Manchester United and as the current captain Gary is the figurehead of the side and thus the obvious target of abuse. But this is not something that bothers him unduly and he will not change his character or beliefs to please the public. At club level, only United supporters appreciate Gary's value to the team, but when he is wearing an England shirt things are very different. Club grievances are put to one side and everyone agrees he is a certainty to start at right-back for the national team. The same fans that cheer for him at Anfield playing for England, try to rip him apart when he arrives in a Manchester United shirt later in the season. He has always been outspoken on a variety of issues, but this is simply Gary Neville being true to himself and his principles. As a result, though, he has upset sections of supporters across the country.

However, his desire to help with charity work is one stance that nobody can argue with; Neville has taken an active part in supporting several charities during his career. In February 2005, he spoke about his role in an Oxfam scheme in Africa. It was a PFA initiative to help children in underprivileged communities, and Gary was quick to get involved. He agreed to donate his Christmas Day salary to Oxfam and encouraged his team-mates to do likewise. As he explained to BBC Sport: 'If we can just help in a little way through our status and through giving a little bit back, that'll be important and affect a lot of people's lives in a positive way.' He has always been keen to support good causes and has joined his United team-mates at UNICEF gala dinners. As a well-paid professional footballer, Neville is usually eager to participate in causes that allow him to give something back to the community and this is yet another reason for Gary being such a good role model for aspiring footballers.

When he finally hangs up his boots at Old Trafford, he will go down as a Manchester United legend. His performances and achievements are as special as any player who has worn the red shirt of United. It would be nice to think he will one day be back at the club in a coaching or managerial capacity, because the supporters love him and he would be a very popular figure at the helm. With his coaching qualifications well underway, it is surely only a matter of time before Gary makes a smooth transition into the world of management. It would be fitting if a playing career that has been so greatly devoted to United led to a managerial spell at the only club he has ever known.

Acknowledgements

I would like to thank Nick Callow and everyone at Hayters Teamwork for all their support and advice and Stuart Robertson at John Blake Publishing for his feedback and patience.

I am also very grateful to Henry Winter for his help and guidance over the last few years.

Lastly I would like to say how much I appreciate the encouragement and understanding of my family, friends and my girlfriend, Melissa.